Notes on the Catechism

An Outline of the Faith

Revised Edition

James C. Thompson

MOREHOUSE-BARLOW

Wilton, Connecticut

ACKNOWLEDGMENTS

Biblical quotations used in this book are from the *Revised Standard Version* of the Bible, copyrighted 1946, 1952 © 1971, 1973. They are used by permission.

The quotation from *Your Confirmation*, by John Stott, is used by permission of the author and Hodder & Stoughton Ltd., publishers.

The quotation from *Christian Believing*, by Robert E. Terwilliger, is used by permission of Morehouse-Barlow Co., Inc.

Material from The Book of Common Prayer has been used in this book as follows:

"An Outline of the Faith, commonly called the Catechism" plus appropriate quotations of other passages as needed. Reprinted by permission.

TABLE OF CONTENTS

Dedicated to
The Rt. Rev. Victor M. Rivera, D.D.
Bishop of San Joaquin
a faithful Father-in-God
and to
Ruth and Les Cooper
outstanding Churchpeople

CHAPTER I

Human Nature

Q. What are we by nature?
A. We are part of God's creation, made in the image of God.

It is important to know who we are. A person who does not know who he is suffers from amnesia, a loss of memory. Such cases are rare. What is much more common is uncertainty as to what we are as human beings. The Catechism provides an answer from the Church's memory of who man is. There are two aspects of this answer. One is that we are a part of God's creation. We are here because a Greater Power intended that we should be. As humans we are a higher form of animal life, but that is not the whole story about us. The second part of the Church's answer is the glory of our existence. We are created in the image of God.

Q. What does it mean to be created in the image of God?
A. It means that we are free to make choices: to love, to create, to reason, and to live in harmony with creation and with God.

The Church's teaching that we are created in the image of God means that we share with our Creator those attributes that have to do with freedom. Our freedom is limited. It is never absolute, but it is always real. We can and do make choices to love, to create, to reason and to live in harmony with God and his creation. The Catechism also implies what the doctrine of the image of God in mankind does not mean. It does not mean that we look like God or that he looks like us. God does not have a human body. He has placed within us certain spiritual qualities, outlined in the Catechism, which we have in common with him.

Q. Why then do we live apart from God and out of harmony with creation?
A. From the beginning, human beings have misused their freedom and made wrong choices.

The Catechism states that we have a problem. We are out of harmony with God and his creation. It assumes that we did not invent this problem, for it is the human problem. For a way in which the Bible states the problem, you may wish to read the story of Adam and Eve in the third chapter of the Book of Genesis.

Q. Why do we not use our freedom as we should?
A. Because we rebel against God, and we put ourselves in the place of God.

Idolatry is the worship of that less than God in the place of God. The human tendency is to worship oneself, to place oneself in the center of all things and to wish that all things would revolve around the self and its wishes. To provide the simplest illustration, who among us has not considered an inconvenient rainstorm a personal affront? The Bible reminds us that only God is worthy of worship, only God is the center of all things, only God is entitled to have all things revolve around him. When we place ourselves at the center, we have misused our freedom and have rebelled against God.

Q. What help is there for us?
A. Our help is in God.

At the heart of the Church's teaching is the conviction that God is and he helps. The remedy for the human problem is the divine help that we call the Christian Gospel.

Q. How did God first help us?
A. God first helped us by revealing himself and his will through nature and history, through many seers and saints, and especially through the prophets of Israel.

This points to God's revelation of himself through nature, the history of nations and especially through a special community, Israel. From the observation of nature, we can see the hint of an intelligence that is greater than ourselves. The specific revelation of the nature of this intelligence, whom we call God, begins in a community, the historic people of Israel.

The Catechism mentions seers and saints and dwells especially upon the prophets. This is a reminder of the words of the Nicene Creed, which says of the Holy Spirit: "He has spoken through the Prophets." The Creed refers to the great prophets of the Old Testament; Isaiah, Jeremiah, Amos, Micah, Hosea and many others. It would also include St. John Baptist, who was the last of the prophets of the old covenant and the herald of the new. Among the saints of the Old Testament were many women. Notable among them were Sarah, Deborah, Ruth, Esther and in The Apocrypha, Susanna.

CHAPTER II

God the Father

Q. What do we learn about God as creator from the revelation to Israel?

A. We learn that there is one God, the Father Almighty, creator of heaven and earth, of all that is, seen and unseen.

The Father is the creator of all, our world, all life and other things upon that world; all universal systems within our galaxy and beyond it. If there are life forms in what we call outer space, we are assured that their creator is the same God who created us. This God is revealed first in the experience of Israel. That revelation is recorded in what we now call the Old Testament and its Apocrypha. The creator of all things is revealed as the lover of all things that he creates. It is his delight that is the motivation for creation. God does not need to create in order to be God. He creates because he delights to do so. You may wish to read the following portions of the Scriptures: Genesis 1:1-2:3, Job 38 and 39, and Psalm 8. A New Testament reference would be St. John 3:16-18.

Q. What does this mean?

A. This means that the universe is good, that it is the work of a single loving God who creates, sustains, and directs it.

The creation story in the first chapter of the Book of Genesis affirms the goodness of the created order. This does not mean that evil does not intrude upon this goodness, but it does mean that the universe as created suits the purpose and delight of God.

Q. What does this mean about our place in the universe?
A. It means that the world belongs to its creator; and that we are called to enjoy it and to care for it in accordance with God's purposes.

The Christian Faith affirms that we are stewards of a creation that belongs to God who called it into being. We do have a responsibility for the wise use of all resources including natural resources. This responsibility is not to be a joyless one, nor is it to be an all consuming passion as if it were the one goal of life. The Churchman is under two obligations: to enjoy and to care. In fact our care can become demonic if we do not enjoy that for which we care. It is a Biblical affirmation that God has given us all things richly to enjoy (I Timothy 6:17).

Q. What does this mean about human life?
A. It means that all people are worthy of respect and honor, because all are created in the image of God, and all can respond to the love of God.

The basic dignity of human life is in the existence of an image of God in every human being. This image may be marred and bent by sin, but it is not wholly absent. The Catechism voices the hope that the Church has even for the "hopeless." The Church has seen enough miracles, enough people turned from disasterous directions, that it can hope as long as life persists.

Q. How was this revelation handed down to us?
A. This revelation was handed down to us through a community created by a covenant with God.

The reference is to the people of Israel. Judaism holds a special place in the affection of the Church. The patriarchs, seers and prophets of Israel are the grandfathers of the Church.

CHAPTER III

The Old Covenant

Q. What is meant by a covenant with God?

A. A covenant is a relationship initiated by God to which a body of people responds in faith.

The Hebrews wished to express the reliability of God in concrete terms. The word "covenant" appears over 200 times in the Bible, and it is a basic idea in the understanding of the Scriptures. In fact the word means the same as the word "testament." The Old Testament is simply the old covenant and the New Testament, the new covenant. A covenant was an agreement between two parties. It was not necessarily an agreement between equals. A treaty between a ruling power and a subject people was referred to as a covenant. The key idea of the Biblical covenant was that God made certain promises which could be depended upon. In return the community promised to follow and obey him. It should also be noted that a lifelong agreement of the most solemn nature between two friends was a covenant. Their heirs had the right to decide whether to continue to participate in the covenant or not. There is a hint of this in the story of David and Jonathan's son, Mephibosheth, in 2 Samuel 9.

Q. What is the Old Covenant?

A. The Old Covenant is the one given by God to the Hebrew people.

When the Hebrews thought about the covenant, they thought primarily about the covenant between God and Israel given to Moses at Mount Sinai. There were earlier covenants between God and Noah and between God and Abraham, but it was the Sinai covenant that was foremost in their minds.

Q. What did God promise them?
A. God promised that they would be his people to bring all the nations of the world to him.

The promise that ". . . in thy seed shall all of the families of the earth be blessed" (Genesis 12:3 K.J.V.) was a persistent element in the Hebrew idea of covenant, coming as it did from the earlier Abrahamic Covenant. A narrower strand in Judaism sought to restrict the benefits of covenant to the Jews alone, but it was with this larger idea that Our Lord identified.

Q. What response did God require from the chosen people?
A. God required the chosen people to be faithful, to love justice, to do mercy, and to walk humbly with their God.

The appropriate response to any covenant or agreement is faithfulness on the part of both parties. God's faithfulness is promised. Israel's faithfulness is required. The phrase, ". . . to love justice, to do mercy, and to walk humbly with their God" is a reference to Micah 6:8. Religion is both a matter of worship and ethics. Above all peoples, the Hebrew people discovered this.

Q. Where is this Old Covenant to be found?
A. The covenant with the Hebrew people is to be found in

the books which we call the Old Testament.

The Old Testament is the written record of the revelation of God to the people of Israel. It will be discussed in the section on the Holy Scriptures.

Q. Where in the Old Testament is God's will for us shown most clearly?

A. God's will for us is shown most clearly in the Ten Commandments.

The Ten Commandments are found in Exodus 20 and in Deuteronomy 5. They are in *The Book of Common Prayer* on pages 317 and 350.

CHAPTER IV

The Ten Commandments

Q. What are the Ten Commandments?
A. The Ten Commandments are the laws given to Moses and
   the people of Israel.

The Ten Commandments are the basis for Mosaic Law in the
Old Testament. They are the foundation of morality in those
civilizations influenced by the Jewish-Christian tradition.
These laws are also known as the Decalogue, which means
ten words.

Q. What do we learn from these commandments?
A. We learn two things: our duty to God, and our duty to
   our neighbors.

The first four Commandments have to do with our duty
toward God. The last six have to do with our duty toward
our neighbors.

Q. What is our duty to God?
A. Our duty is to believe and trust in God;

   I To love and obey God and to bring others to know
     him;

II To put nothing in the place of God;

III To show God respect in thought, word, and deed;

IV And to set aside regular times for worship, prayer, and the study of God's ways.

It is to be noted that the Roman numerals opposite the answers in this and the next question designate the number of the commandment to which the answer refers.

The Catechism speaks freely of our duty. No society can long survive without those who know their duty and do it. No spiritual life can survive without a willingness in the matter of duty.

Christian duty is joyful in that it is born of faith. Faith's end is the vision of God, and, therefore, it participates in the joy that comes from the quest for that vision. Christian duty is nonetheless duty. The Catechism tells us plainly that our first duty is to God. It is to believe and trust in him, to love and obey him, and to bring others to know him. In connection with this latter obligation, it should be said that the most effective witness to God will be enthusiasm for the Faith and the Church. Our duty to God is to put nothing in his place. This is the sin of idolatry. It would be odd for any of us to be tempted to bow down to a carved idol in this day and age. This is not our temptation. A far more basic human temptation is ours, however: We do put self at the center of our devotion in a multitude of ways.

We are to honor God's Name and his Word by the cultivation of an attitude of respect. "The fear of the Lord," so often mentioned in the Bible, is simply reverence.

A regular time for worship is one of our obligations. Except in extraordinary circumstances, this will be on Sunday. A regular time for prayer as an individual, quite apart from the corporate worship of the Church, is required for the health of the Christian soul. The study of God's ways would include the study of the Scriptures and the observation of God's ways in nature and human personality.

Q. What is our duty to our neighbors?
A. Our duty to our neighbors is to love them as ourselves, and to do to other people as we wish them to do to us.

    V To love, honor, and help our parents and family; to honor those in authority, and to meet their just demands;

   VI To show respect for the life God has given us; to work and pray for peace; to bear no malice, prejudice, or hatred in our hearts; and to be kind to all the creatures of God;

  VII To use all our bodily desires as God intended;

 VIII To be honest and fair in our dealings; to seek justice, freedom, and the necessities of life for all people; and to use our talents and possessions as ones who must answer for them to God.

   IX To speak the truth, and not to mislead others by our silence;

    X To resist temptations to envy, greed, and jealousy; to rejoice in other people's gifts and graces; and to do our duty for the love of God, who has called us into fellowship with him.

Our first duty is to God; our second is to our neighbor. We are to love our neighbor as ourselves. The Bible assumes that we are free to love others if we rightly value ourselves. If we doubt our own value as persons, we project our negative feelings about ourselves on others. The direction to do unto others as we wish them to do unto us (St. Matthew 7:12) assumes that we are healthy in our feelings about ourselves, and that we know what we really want done unto us by others.

The family is our nearest neighbor. It is difficult to remember this at times. Sometimes we presume upon the tolerance and forgiveness of the family. It is a good thing that tolerance and forgiveness are often there in good measure. It would be helpful for us to accord the same courtesy we give to friends and strangers to the members of our own families.

The Christian has always had the greatest respect for the civil authority, even in those times and places where the civil authority has not been Christian. In this connection you may wish to read Romans 13:1-7. Of course, it is much easier for a Christian to obey the laws in a constitutional democracy than it is under certain other kinds of government. It is easier for a Christian to obey the laws in societies that take a positive attitude toward the Churches. The demands of civil authority are to be met unless they conflict with the positive commandments of divine law. If we find ourselves in a situation where we must obey God rather than men, we must honor the civil authority by first exhausting all legal remedies that are provided to protect both our rights and our consciences. Should these remedies fail, we ought to be prepared to accept the consequences for such disobedience.

Our duty to our neighbor calls for respect for human life, and it is concerned with social and international relationships as well as personal ones.

Our duty to our neighbor includes the right use of our bodily desires. The seventh commandment itself is concerned with a right use of sexual desire. This is liable to misuse as is any desire. We must understand that desire in and of itself is a good thing and quite necessary to the fulfillment of human life. However, any desire can get out of hand and become destructive, in which case it becomes a sinful desire. At Baptism we renounce the sinful desires that draw us from the love of God. Lust differs from love in that it is largely sexually exploitive and cannot assume real responsibility for the other. As biblical religion developed, it upheld sexual loyalty to one partner. In the Prayer Book, please read THE ORDER FOR THE CELEBRATION AND BLESSING OF A MARRIAGE, p. 423 ff. In marriage the negative tone of the Seventh Commandment is upheld and transcended by the positive and joyful relationship of mutual fidelity. This is true of faithful marriage in later Jewish and all Christian teaching. As a sign of God's uncovenanted mercy it is true of faithful marriage in other religions and in those of secular bent.

Our duty to our neighbor calls for integrity in all our dealings with him, and beyond that, a positive seeking of his good. The use of our own abilities and possessions as those who will answer to God for them is part of our duty to our neighbor. We are to respect the truth and speak it. A silence that misleads deliberately can be as wrong as an outright falsehood in certain situations.

To covet is to desire that which is the legitimate possession of another in such a way that theft is prevented only by a consideration of consequences. To admire another's possession is quite a different thing. For example, we may admire a neighbor's car and wish that we had one just like it without any desire to take it from him. Presumably we could buy one just like it if we wished.

Envy is a danger to the spiritual life, for when we envy, we resent the possessions or attainments of another person; and so come to hate that person. The Catechism teaches us that we are to rejoice in other people's gifts and graces. That way we add to our happiness and theirs as well.

These things are a duty that can be done for the love of

God, who has called us into fellowship with himself in Jesus Christ our Lord.

Q. What is the purpose of the Ten Commandments?
A. The Ten Commandments were given to define our relationship with God and our neighbors.

The Ten Commandments describe what love looks like. They describe the outward behavior of one who loves God and his neighbor. That is the purpose of the Commandments. They do not automatically produce one who loves both God and neighbor.

Q. Since we do not fully obey them, are they useful at all?
A. Since we do not fully obey them, we see more clearly our sin and our need for redemption.

The Ten Commandments are a large order for mankind. When we ask how we are going to accomplish all this, and when we ask what do we do when we fail, we are ready to discover the deeper meaning of the Christian Faith. The Faith deals with us at the point that we fail. It says that we cannot earn our way into God's favor. We need a Savior. It is the Savior that Christianity offers.

CHAPTER V

Sin and Redemption

Q. What is sin?

A. Sin is the seeking of our own will instead of the will of God, thus distorting our relationship with God, with other people, and with all creation.

In the New Testament the word for sin is a term from archery which means to miss the mark. When we miss the mark that God has set for us as human beings, we sin. Commonly, theologians make a number of distinctions in the use of the word "sin." A primary distinction is between original sin and actual sin. Original sin is manifest in the human tendency to place self before God. The remedy is the grace of Holy Baptism. Actual sin is traditionally thought of as two in kind, mortal and venial.

Mortal sins are both deliberate and grave in nature. They seriously disturb our relationship to God. Traditionally, there are seven mortal or deadly sins: Pride, Anger, Covetousness, Lust, Envy, Sloth and Gluttony. These are all corruptions of good impulses. Pride is a sense of self-worth that has grown out of proportion to reality. Lust is love that is out of control . . . so also for each of the deadly sins. Evil is always a corruption of some good.

Venial sins are those that are committed carelessly, that is to say, without conscious intent, and are lesser in nature than mortal sins.

The remedy for all sins committed after Baptism is to be found in repentance, confession and absolution. Further material on the reconciliation of a penitent can be found in the section on other sacramental rites.

Q. How does sin have power over us?
A. Sin has power over us because we lose our liberty when our relationship with God is distorted.

In Christ, we have been made free. In this connection you may wish to read St. John 8:32-36. In a paradox, true freedom is to be found in the service of God. When sin disturbs this relationship with God, we are in the power of that sin. We love God less, and our relationship to him is inevitably distorted. Persistence in this state will result in the destruction of our relationship to God.

Q. What is redemption?
A. Redemption is the act of God which sets us free from the power of evil, sin, and death.

Redemption is deliverance. It is an idea that comes from the Old Testament. Its probable origin is in the obligation of the near-kinsman to deliver one who is in trouble. The idea is that we are in trouble, and God acts as our kinsman. The story of God's action is the story of the Gospel.

Q. How did God prepare us for redemption?
A. God sent the prophets to call us back to himself, to show us our need for redemption, and to announce the coming of the Messiah.

The Old Testament, as seen from Christian eyes, is the story of God's preparation of humanity for the Gospel. The key to this activity is to be found in the work of the prophets. Proclaiming a message of both personal and social righteousness, they measured their society and themselves against the intention of God for mankind.

Q. What is meant by the Messiah?
A. The Messiah is one sent by God to free us from the power of sin, so that with the help of God we may live in harmony with God, within ourselves, with our neighbors, and with all creation.

The Christian idea of the Messiah is a development of the Old Testament idea of the Messiah. The Messiah in Judaism was thought of as a heaven-sent prince who would deliver God's people from their enemies. In Christianity, the Messiah delivers us from our ultimate enemies. These are defined in a previous question as the power of evil, sin, and death.

Q. Who do we believe is the Messiah?
A. The Messiah, or Christ, is Jesus of Nazareth, the only Son of God.

Messiah and Christ have the same meaning. The first word is Hebrew; the second is Greek. Christians identify the Christ as Jesus of Nazareth. Jesus is the only Son of God in that it is his nature. We are the children of God by adoption and grace.

CHAPTER VI

God the Son

Q. What do we mean when we say that Jesus is the only Son of God?

A. We mean that Jesus is the only perfect image of the Father, and shows us the nature of God.

This section concerns the most important person in our lives, Jesus Christ, the Son of God. He is far more than an historical character, who lived in an obscure corner of the Roman Empire 2000 years ago. St. Paul teaches that Christ is the image of the invisible God (Colossians 1:15). Another way of putting it would be that Jesus is the human face of God. In what Jesus was, we find what God is.

Q. What is the nature of God revealed in Jesus?
A. God is love.

Jesus of Nazareth acted toward persons in a way that sought their own best good. This does not mean that he was too "soft" or overly sentimental about people. He demanded the best from each person. He could be hard on those who failed to live up to their own best. With respect to compassion, Jesus showed more pity for those who failed God through the weakness of the flesh than for those whose sins proceeded from a want of charitableness.

   The statement that God is love is implied in a number of places in the Bible, and is specifically stated in I John 4:16. That God is love is revealed supremely in the life of Jesus.

Q. What do we mean when we say that Jesus was conceived by the power of the Holy Spirit and became incarnate from the Virgin Mary?

A. We mean that by God's own act, his divine Son received our human nature from the Virgin Mary, his mother.

The doctrine or dogma of the Incarnation means that the coming of the Son of God in Jesus of Nazareth was the will of the Father. The Incarnation was not by human will or a result of chance in the processes of biological reproduction. It was the will and action of the First Person of the Holy Trinity that the Second Person of the Holy Trinity become incarnate in the person of Jesus of Nazareth. Having said this, we do take note of the Scriptural tradition that the assent of the will of the Blessed Virgin Mary was necessary in order that God's will be done. In this connection, you may wish to read the account of the Annunciation, St. Luke 1:26-38. Pay close attention to the final verse of this passage.

   To believe this is to believe that which is the doctrine of the Incarnation. This is the theological dogma. The biological question ought to be considered separately. It is possible for intelligent Christians to believe in a literal Virgin Birth. It is a fact also that other intelligent Christians, equally devoted to our Lord, do not believe in a literal Virgin Birth. The whole question may be put in perspective when we realize that it is mentioned only by St. Matthew and St. Luke in the first part of the Gospels and does not appear again in the New Testament. That Jesus is the Son of God is the firm conviction of every New Testament writer. We must take seriously the Church's teaching that Jesus was fully human and fully divine.

The insight of the letter to the Hebrews that: ". . . we have not a high priest, who is unable to sympathize with our weaknesses, but one who in every respect has been tempted as we are, yet without sin. Let us then with confidence draw near to the throne of grace, that we may receive mercy and find grace to help in time of need" (4:15-16) ought to be an encouragement to us. At the same time, we ought to understand that Jesus in his humanity stood where we have so often broken and run. If we get to Heaven, it will be because our imperfect lives are joined with the perfect offering of his own life (Eucharistic Prayer B, p. 369, B.C.P.). We are totally dependent upon the grace of God through Jesus Christ our Lord.

Q. Why did he take our human nature?
A. The divine Son became human, so that in him human beings might be adopted as children of God, and be made heirs of God's kingdom.

The Incarnation is an act of the love of God. The God of the New Testament does not thunder his decrees from on high. Rather, he comes among us as Jesus of Nazareth.

The best exposition of this question in the Catechism is to be found in one of the Scriptural words that follow the Absolution in Holy Eucharist I, a quotation from St. John 3:16:

God so loved the world that he gave his only-begotten Son, to the end that all that believe in him should not perish, but have everlasting life.

Q. What is the great importance of Jesus' suffering and death?
A. By his obedience, even to suffering and death, Jesus made the offering which we could not make; in him we are freed from the power of sin and reconciled to God.

The Christ is the Redeemer. This is a title that is applied to God many times in the Old Testament. As has been pointed out, the word involves the idea of one who rescues a kinsman. The New Testament teaches that Christ died for our sins. In this connection you will want to read the following Scriptures: Romans 5:6; I Corinthians 15:3 and St. Matthew 20:28 and St. Mark 10:45.

There are a number of senses in which it is true that Christ died for our sins. It was human sin that accomplished the death of our Lord. We share in the very same sins that brought Christ to the Cross. We must remember that the chief characters in the drama of the crucifixion—Annas, Caiaphas and Pontius Pilate—were not monsters devoid of human feeling. If we would dress them in modern attire, they would not be so different from us. In fact they might resemble us too much. It was "blindness of heart, pride, vainglory, and hypocrisy . . . envy, hatred and malice" (The Great Litany) that nailed God's Son to the Cross. We have these problems still. The Faith teaches us that it was because we humans have these problems that God sent his only Son, even when that sending meant the Cross. The crucifixion of Jesus is our human "no" to God. At the Cross, Jesus takes upon himself that sin and that rejection. This is not only the choice of God the Father; it is also the choice of the Son. The thieves crucified with Jesus had no choice. They had been captured, and were sent to the crosses that Roman justice provided for them. Jesus could have avoided the Cross. He knew that going to Jerusalem at that time involved the risk: yes, the inevitability of the Cross. He could have stayed in Galilee. It is conjecture, of course; but perhaps even in Jerusalem, he could have reached a compromise with the Jewish authorities. There is a further consideration — one that we may well neglect in our sophistication. St. Matthew 26:53 says that at the time of our

Lord's arrest he knew that he could call on twelve legions of angels. This would mean 72,000, far more angels than the Roman procurator had soldiers. Our Lord was symbolizing in terms that those familiar with Roman legions would understand a tremendous power. Jesus chose to go to the Cross.

The Catechism emphasizes the obedience of our Lord. His sacrifice of his life is the oblation of a perfect life that we cannot offer. Alone he has fulfilled the intention of God for human life, and God accepts the offering of that life. Our imperfect offerings are now acceptable when joined with his one perfect sacrifice.

Q. What is the significance of Jesus' resurrection?
A. By his resurrection, Jesus overcame death and opened for us the way of eternal life.

The power of a cross is the power of death; the power of sin is identical. Sin dulls our capacity for any kind of relationship to God and then kills that capacity. Our Lord suffered in his body the penalty that is the soul's penalty for sin. The Gospel is that at the cross Jesus broke the power of sin and death. The grave could not hold him. Easter Day is God's "yes" to our human "no." This feast of Christ's Resurrection is the Queen of Feasts. It is a time when all the faithful will make a special effort to be present at the Eucharist and to receive their Easter communion. Without Easter, the story of Jesus is a dismal failure. Easter is central to our faith. Let us be careful to observe it. Let us also remember that every Lord's Day is a remembrance of Easter and should be honored.

Q. What do we mean when we say that he descended to the dead?
A. We mean that he went to the departed and offered them also the benefits of redemption.

The question of those who had died before the coming of Christ arose very early in the Church. St. Peter gives the answer of a very early strand in the Christian tradition when he says that after the Lord's death, he preached to the spirits in prison. St. Peter means that the Gospel was then offered to the departed. You may wish to read I St. Peter 3:18-20 and 4:6.

Q. What do we mean when we say that he ascended into heaven and is seated at the right hand of the Father?
A. We mean that Jesus took our human nature into heaven where he now reigns with the Father and intercedes for us.

The exaltation of our Lord is marked by the Ascension Day, which is forty days after Easter Day. The New Testament teaches that the resurrected Christ did not remain on earth, but that after a period of further instruction for the disciples, he returned to the Father to make way for the coming of the Holy Spirit.

The Apostles' Creed says:

He ascended into heaven,
    and is seated at the right hand of the Father.

The imagery is that of the oriental court, with the right hand the place of honor. The Catechism teaches that the Lord took our human nature into heaven. Christ the King reigns as our brother. The humanity of the Son is not discarded at the Ascension, but accompanies him into heaven, where his work is to intercede for us, his brothers.

Q. How can we share in his victory over sin, suffering, and death?
A. We share in his victory when we are baptized into the New Covenant and become living members of Christ.

Holy Baptism is the sacrament that incorporates us into the Church, which is the Body of Christ. Thus we participate with him in the benefits of his Passion, Death and Resurrection.

CHAPTER VII

The New Covenant

Q. What is the New Covenant?

A. The New Covenant is the new relationship with God given by Jesus Christ, the Messiah, to the apostles; and through them, to all who believe in him.

The prophet Jeremiah spoke of a time when God would make a new covenant with Israel. You may wish to read Jeremiah 31:31-34 in this connection. This New Covenant was given by Jesus Christ to the Apostles, and through them to all the faithful. It replaces the Mosaic or Old Covenant. The Church is understood to be the New Israel of God.

Q. What did the Messiah promise in the New Covenant?

A. Christ promised to bring us into the kingdom of God and give us life in all its fullness.

The Kingdom of God was an important concept to Jesus and the Apostles. The ancient Jews thought of this kingdom as the sphere of God's rule. That rule took place in three dimensions: (1) God is the ruler of nature. "Heaven is my throne and the earth is my footstool . . ." (Isaiah 66:1). (2) God will be the ruler of the future—the kingdom that is coming. In this regard you may wish to consult the following references: Isaiah, chapters 11-13 and 34:1-8; Obadiah 1:15-21; Micah 4:1-8 and Zephaniah 3:8-13. This is the time when God will triumph over all opposition and all evil, and his kingdom will be in the midst of his people. This is the time to which the New Testament looks forward as the time in which "The kingdom of the world has become the kingdom of our Lord and of his Christ, and he shall reign forever and ever" (Revelation 11:15b). (3) God is the ruler of the individual who takes upon himself the yoke of the kingdom. It is in this third sense, that the kingdom of God is related to the present through our own experience.

Jesus brings us into the kingdom of God. To obey him is to enter into God's present kingdom. The kingdom of God's triumph is promised to us also. We will not be excluded from it or its benefits.

In the Gospel of St. John, our Lord says: "I came that they may have life, and have it abundantly" (10:10b). Christ does not want to destroy anything that is positive in our lives. He wants to add to it and add abundantly.

Q. What response did Christ require?
A. Christ commanded us to believe in him and to keep his commandments.

Jesus said, ". . . believe in God, believe also in me" (St. John 14:1b). There are two senses in which we believe. One is to believe that something exists. I believe that a certain place exists or that a certain concept is true. My beliefs may or may not make a difference to my life. The second is to believe in something. I not only believe that my kitchen ladder exists, but also I trust it to hold my weight. This does make a difference to my life. This is faith, and this is the kind of belief that Jesus asked us to have in him.

The second part of the requirement mentioned by the Catechism is to keep our Lord's commandments. It would be inconsistent to believe in Jesus as the Son of God and our Savior and to distain his commandments.

Q. What are the commandments taught by Christ?
A. Christ taught us the Summary of the Law and gave us the New Commandment.

In the Prayer Book, the Summary of the Law is said following the Collect for Purity in Holy Eucharist I. The Ten Commandments may be substituted for it. It is found in St. Matthew 22:37-40. It is also found in A PENITENTIAL ORDER: RITE II, p. 351. The form used there is from Mark 12:29-31. The New Commandment is found in St. John 13:34-35.

Q. What is the Summary of the Law?
A. You shall love the Lord your God with all your heart, with all your soul, and with all your mind. This is the first and the great commandment. And the second is like it: You shall love your neighbor as yourself.

The Law of Christ requires both love of God and love of neighbor. The Christian is under the same obligation with regard to love as were the people of the Old Covenant.

Q. What is the New Commandment?
A. The New Commandment is that we love one another as Christ loved us.

Nothing seems more useless than a command to love. This is because love is for us a feeling. The Greek language, which is the language of the New Testament, had a more extensive vocabulary with regard to love. There was a word for love between a man and a woman, sexual love. There was a word that signified the love that was appreciation or friendship. There was a word, rare outside the New Testament, that meant acting toward another with a desire for their own best good. It is in this latter sense that we can be commanded to love. Although it may be accompanied by feelings, it is not so much feeling as it is good will. The love of Christ is able to encompass that which is not love in us. Our response to that love ought to be a similar good will toward our neighbor.

Q. Where may we find what Christians believe about Christ?
A. What Christians believe about Christ is found in the Scriptures and summed up in the creeds.

Our Church is a creedal Church. The Episcopal Church in the United States and its sister Churches in the Anglican Communion refer to the historic Creeds, which are a summary of the teaching of the Holy Scriptures. The creedal reference to the divinity and humanity of Christ, his life, death, resurrection, ascension and final advent are what the Catechism means when it says that the Church's belief about Christ is summed up in the Creeds.

The Creeds are summaries of Christian teaching, and, as will be seen, not complete statements about the whole range of Christian teaching. For a total picture of Christian belief, one must look further. Traditional bases of belief for the Episcopal Church are the Holy Scriptures, Tradition and Reason. Some would say that belief is further tested by Conscience and Christian Experience.

Certain other Churches, particularly those rooted in the Protestant Reformation, state their beliefs in documents known as Confessions of Faith, and are sometimes called Confessional Churches. Other groups, far more recent in history, depend on less formal documents or simply on the Bible alone.

CHAPTER VIII

The Creeds

Q. What are the creeds?
A. The creeds are statements of our basic beliefs about God.

Creed is from a Latin word *credo*, which means, "I believe."
The Creeds outline the basic beliefs of the Church. They do
not say everything. Many concepts and practices which are
of the greatest importance to Christianity are omitted. In the
Creeds used by the Episcopal Church in its worship, you will
find no mention of either the Holy Eucharist or prayer. Those
are certainly things of supreme importance to the Christian
Faith and life. Creeds do state in brief form the foundation
convictions of the Church.

Q. How many creeds does this Church use in its worship?
A. This Church uses two creeds: The Apostles' Creed and the
   Nicene Creed.

By this Church, the Catechism refers to the Episcopal Church
in the United States. Other Churches in the Anglican Communion, of which we are a part, use the Athanasian Creed as
well. That Creed will be discussed in the material that
follows.

Q. What is the Apostles' Creed?
A. The Apostles' Creed is the ancient creed of Baptism; it is
     used in the Church's daily worship to recall our Baptismal
     Covenant.

The Apostles' Creed, in its original and subsequent forms,
was used by Baptismal candidates to confess their faith. We
use this creed in Baptism and in Morning and Evening Prayer.
In the latter services the Creed is a daily reminder of our
Baptism. In as much as this Creed is related to Baptism, it is
the Creed that is appropriate for the Service of the Burial of
the Dead.

Q. What is the Nicene Creed?
A. The Nicene Creed is the creed of the universal Church and
     is used at the Eucharist.

The Nicene Creed was written in the fourth century, A.D., to
make clear what the whole Church believed. "We believe . . ."
is the original form of wording at the beginning of the Creed.
This is particularly fitting for the Holy Eucharist, which must
be a corporate service. In Anglicanism, the rule has been that
while anyone may say the Offices of Morning and Evening
Prayer alone, the Eucharist requires at least two persons, a
Priest and one other communicant.

Q. What, then, is the Athanasian Creed?
A. The Athanasian Creed is an ancient document proclaiming
     the nature of the Incarnation and of God as Trinity.

Included in the English Prayer Book and the Prayer Books of
most, if not all, of our sister Churches is the Athanasian Creed.
It was composed in Latin rather than Greek and is also
known as the *Quicumque Vult.* The American Church did
not choose to use this Creed in its worship since all that is in it
is either stated or implied in the Apostles' and Nicene Creeds.

It is most specific concerning the doctrines of the Incarnation and the Holy Trinity.

Whenever this Creed is used in the worship of other Anglican Churches, it is substituted for the Apostles' Creed in Morning Prayer. It is an occasional substitution, however, and not used each day or each Sunday.

One of the reasons that the Athanasian Creed has never proved as popular for use in worship as the other Creeds is because it contains certain "damnatory clauses." It might be well to quote from the Book of Common Prayer of the Canadian Church with regard to this Creed:

For the removal of doubts, and to prevent disquietude in the use of the Creed commonly called the Creed of Saint Athanasius, it is solemnly declared:

1. That the Confession of our Christian Faith, commonly called the Creed of Saint Athanasius, does not make any additions to the Faith as contained in holy Scripture, but warns against errors which from time to time have arisen in the Church of Christ.

2. That as holy Scripture in divers places promises life to them that believe, and declares the condemnation of them that believe not, so the Church in this Confession declares the necessity for all who would be in a state of salvation, of holding fast the Catholic Faith, and the great peril of rejecting the same. Wherefore the warnings in this Confession of Faith are to be understood not otherwise than the like warnings in holy Scripture; for we must receive God's threatenings, even as his promises, in such wise as they are generally set forth in holy Writ. Moreover, the Church does not herein pronounce a judgment on any particular person or persons, God alone being the Judge of all.[1]

[1] *Book of Common Prayer*-Anglican Church of Canada. 1959. p. 698.

Q. What is the Trinity?

A. The Trinity is one God: Father, Son and Holy Spirit.

Christianity in common with its parent religion, Judaism, believes in one God. Certain other faiths, notably Islam, also believe in one God. A major difference between Christianity and other monotheistic religions is that Christians believe that the one God is a Trinity in Unity. The Church does not believe in three gods, but it does believe that the one God is at the same time, Father, Son and Holy Spirit. This belief arose out of the ways in which the early Christians experienced the reality of God. This is summed up by the Rev. J. R. W. Stott, who writes:

First, the doctrine of the Trinity is not a peculiar theory invented by unpractical theologians; it is an attempt to put into words a truth which God revealed in facts of *history*. Let me explain. The apostles were Jews who had been brought up to believe in God, the Creator of the world and the Holy One of Israel. Then they met Jesus, and as they lived with Him, they came to realize that He was no mere man. He was divine. Yet He was not himself the Father, for He used to pray to the Father. Then He started telling them of Someone else, whom He called 'the Spirit of Truth' and 'the Paraclete' or 'Comforter', who would come and take His place when He had gone. On the Day of Pentecost this Holy Spirit did come with the fullness of divine power. But He was not the Father. Nor was He Jesus, who had now ascended to the Father's right hand. He was one with Them, and yet He was distinct from Them. So it was the pressure of their own experience which forced the apostles to believe in the Trinity.[2]

---

[2]J. R. W. Stott, *Your Confirmation*, London: Hodder and Stoughton, 1958. p. 51.

In this same chapter, Dr. Stott makes the point that we are often confused by the doctrine of the Trinity because we do not understand the difference between a mathematical trinity and an organic trinity. The Holy Trinity is an organic trinity, not a mathematical one.

CHAPTER IX

The Holy Spirit

Q. Who is the Holy Spirit?
A. The Holy Spirit is the Third Person of the Trinity, God at work in the world and in the Church even now.

As the Father is God present in the processes of creation, and as Christ is God present in the Incarnation; so the Holy Spirit is God present in the world and in the Church. While it is true that God is at work in both world and Church, it is also true that it is in the Church that he is recognized as God and given the worship that is his right.

Q. How is the Holy Spirit revealed in the Old Covenant?
A. The Holy Spirit is revealed in the Old Covenant as the giver of life, the One who spoke through the prophets.

A specific reference is to the story in Genesis that puts the Spirit in the beginning of creation as one who moves over the face of the waters. It is the Genesis tradition that God's Spirit abides with man the days of his life (Genesis 6:3). The prophets are considered to have exercised their authority as interpreters of history through the Spirit of God. The Old Testament is not without a doctrine of the Spirit, but it is in

the New Testament that the Spirit is revealed as a person
within the Godhead.

Q. How is the Holy Spirit revealed in the New Covenant?
A. The Holy Spirit is revealed as the Lord who leads us into
   all truth and enables us to grow in the likeness of Christ.

In the New Testament the deepest understanding of the Holy
Spirit is afforded by the Gospel of St. John. In that Gospel the
Lord promises the Apostles that when the Spirit comes he will
guide them into all truth (St. John 16:13). Note that this is a
promise to the Church as a corporate body and is made to its
leaders, the Apostles, whom our bishops succeed in office. It
is as we follow the teachings of the Church that we are guided
into all truth. It is the "Apostles' teaching and fellowship"
that is important here. The Catechism emphasizes a second
aspect: the work of the Holy Spirit in enabling us to grow in
the Christian life so that we come to resemble our Lord more
and more. The final realization of the likeness of Christ
awaits the Coming of the Lord. See I John 3:2 in this connection.

Q. How do we recognize the presence of the Holy Spirit in
   our lives?
A. We recognize the presence of the Holy Spirit when we
   confess Jesus Christ as Lord and are brought into love and
   harmony with God, with ourselves, with our neighbors,
   and with all creation.

St. Paul says that the confession of Jesus as Lord is the work
of the Holy Spirit (I Corinthians 12:3b). He points also to
certain fruits of the Spirit which make for love and harmony
with God, ourselves, our neighbors and all creation (Galatians 5:22-23).

It is the teaching of the Prayer Book that the existence of goodness within us is the action of God. You may wish to see the following Collects: Lent 3, Proper 5 and Proper 19. Thus we may conclude that human goodness is itself a sign of the activity of the Holy Spirit.

Q. How do we recognize the truths taught by the Holy Spirit?
A. We recognize truths to be taught by the Holy Spirit when they are in accord with the Scriptures.

We must recognize that one of the aspects of Christian renewal in our Church and in others has been a rediscovery of a personal relationship to Jesus Christ through an intense awareness of the presence and guidance of the Holy Spirit. When this means an increase of faith, hope and charity and a heightened devotion to the Lord's Church as well as to the Lord himself, it is to be welcomed. Having said this one must recognize that there is no Christian belief more subject to serious misinterpretation than the belief in the Holy Spirit. The Catechism rightly tests whatever may be claimed for the Holy Spirit against an objective standard, the teachings of the Holy Scriptures. There are many people who use the Holy Spirit as a justification for their own personal and doctrinal oddities. The Churchman must remember that God is the God of order, not disorder. The doctrine of the Spirit is associated with Wisdom and all that flows from Wisdom: sanity, reasonableness and reverence. The Spirit does indeed move where he wills, but that will is not capricious. He is the divine agent of the Incarnation, is present at the Baptism of our Lord, launches the holy catholic Church at Pentecost, and presides at the Council of the Apostles, so much so that they can say of their decision, ". . . it has seemed good to the Holy Spirit and to us . . ." (Acts 15:28). He is present at every Baptism and every Eucharist. It is by the Church's Scriptures that we recognize the truths taught by the Holy Spirit.

CHAPTER X

The Holy Scriptures

Q. What are the Holy Scriptures?

A. The Holy Scriptures, commonly called the Bible, are the books of the Old and New Testaments; other books, called the Apocrypha, are often included in the Bible.

Christianity is a relationship to a Person. It is Jesus Christ who is the supreme revelation or disclosure of God. For our knowledge of this Person and the Old Covenant that prepared for him and the New Covenant that he instituted, we depend in large measure upon written documents, the Holy Scriptures.

Holy Scriptures are sacred writings. The word, Bible, comes from a word meaning papyrus or book. The Bible consists of sixty-six books; thirty-nine in the Old Testament and twenty-seven in the New Testament. There are fourteen books in the Apocrypha.

Q. What is the Old Testament?

A. The Old Testament consists of books written by the people of the Old Covenant, under the inspiration of the Holy Spirit, to show God at work in nature and history.

The Old Testament accepted by the Church is identical to the Bible of the Hebrew religion. These books, written over a period of 800 years, often incorporate much older material. They are concerned with the interpretation of God as creator and as the Lord of history.

Q. What is the New Testament?
A. The New Testament consists of books written by the people of the New Covenant, under the inspiration of the Holy Spirit, to set forth the life and teachings of Jesus and to proclaim the Good News of the Kingdom for all people.

The New Testament was written over a period of less than 100 years. It is concerned with God as revealed in the life and teachings of Jesus and with proclaiming the Good News of his kingdom which is to be for all mankind. The word, gospel, means good news. It is used in two senses. It may mean the whole of the Christian message or it may refer to one of the written narratives of the life of our Lord. Within the Eucharist, the Gospel is a passage of Scripture read from one of the four Gospels.

Q. What is the Apocrypha?
A. The Apocrypha is a collection of additional books written by people of the Old Covenant and used in the Christian Church.

The fourteen books of the Apocrypha, some of which are accepted by the Roman Church as Scripture in the fullest sense, are considered by the Anglican Communion to be valuable for reading, but they are not thought to be on quite the same level as the other books of the Bible in that no doctrine may be established from them (*Articles of Religion,* VI).

These books, composed in Greek, and written in a period

that may be dated roughly from 180 B.C. to 120 A.D., were accepted as sacred writings by Jews deeply influenced by Greek culture. They were not so accepted by the more conservative Jews, especially those living in Palestine. Many early Christians, including several of the Church Fathers, regularly quoted from the Apocrypha as Holy Scripture.

It was the decision of the Church of England in the early part of the Reformation to limit the Old Testament to those books allowed as Scripture by the Jewish synod of Jamnia in 90 A.D.

The Apocrypha has a deuterocanonical status. The recognition that there were two canons of the Old Testament was common in the Middle Ages. At the Council of Trent the Roman Church abolished the distinction between the Old Testament and the Apocrypha. We continue the understanding of the place of the Apocrypha that characterized the Early and Medieval Churches.

The Episcopal Church does read from the Apocrypha on occasion, substituting the Apocryphal lesson for the Old Testament lesson. It does so because the Apocrypha contains much profound religious wisdom consistent with the Old and New Testaments and much religious history.

You may wish to own a copy of the Bible with Apocrypha. They are available, but you will have to ask for such Bibles by full title. As an alternative you might purchase a copy of the Apocrypha alone.

Q. Why do we call the Holy Scriptures the Word of God?
A. We call them the Word of God because God inspired their human authors and because God still speaks to us through the Bible.

Jesus Christ is the Word Incarnate. The Holy Scriptures are

the Word as written. We worship the Word who is God, not the Book. The Book is important because God used its human authors over a period of many centuries to record and bear witness to his acts in history. Especially do they bear witness to that supreme revelation of God in the Incarnate Lord.

The Anglican Faith has no doctrine of infallibility that applies to any book or Church official. Infallibility belongs to God alone. The Church does have a doctrine of inspiration by which it means enlightenment and guidance. It believes that the authors of Holy Scripture were enlightened and guided by the Holy Spirit. This guidance was without any violation of their own personalities. They were not the mechanical instrument of the Holy Spirit in the same sense that a typewriter is the mechanical instrument of the author.

It might be helpful to remember that God's revelation begins with an action. That action receives a response from those who are the people of God. Within the response is the interpretation of the action that the community, guided by the Holy Spirit, places upon the action. In order for the community to preserve its memory of God's mighty acts and their meaning, a member of the community writes. The community recognizes the writing as consistent with its own teaching and finally deems the writing to be Holy Scripture.

The contemporary proof of the inspiration of the Bible is that through its pages God continues to speak his Word to us.

Q. How do we understand the meaning of the Bible?
A. We understand the meaning of the Bible by the help of the Holy Spirit, who guides the Church in the true interpretation of the Scriptures.

It is the Holy Spirit, who enlightened and guided the authors

of the Bible, who is still guiding the Church in the true interpretation of the Scriptures. It is important for us to remember
that the Bible is the Church's Book. The Church will guide us
in the reading of the Bible by providing sound commentary.
The Holy Spirit will then illuminate our minds and hearts so
that the Bible will become alive for us.

The Episcopal Church is a Church of the Bible. The language of its worship is largely the language of the Scriptures.
Psalter and Bible lessons are the heart of Morning and Evening Prayer. In the Eucharist the Liturgy of the Word precedes
the Liturgy of the Table, teaching us that we feast on the
Scripture as well as on the Sacrament. It was the Church of
England that gave us the Authorized or King James Version
of the Bible in 1611. Anglican scholars continue to make
significant contributions to all major modern revisions and
translations.

CHAPTER XI

The Church

Q. What is the Church?
A. The Church is the community of the New Covenant.

The Church is a body of people. It is people related to God and one another through their participation in the New Covenant. The Thirty-Nine Articles says of the Church:

> The visible Church of Christ is a congregation of faithful men, in which the pure Word of God is preached, and the Sacraments be duly ministered according to Christ's ordinance, in all those things that of necessity are requisite to the same. (Article XIX)

This has the merit of defining the visible Church as faithful people in relationship to the Word and Sacraments of the Covenant.

Q. How is the Church described in the Bible?
A. The Church is described as the Body of which Jesus Christ is the Head and of which all baptized persons are members. It is called the People of God, the new Israel, a holy nation, a royal priesthood, and the pillar and ground of truth.

The Scriptures are extravagant in the terms with which they describe the Church. It must be remembered that the Holy Spirit who inspired the authors of the New Testament was the same Spirit who came at Pentecost to preside at the birth of the Church. The New Testament writers are all Churchmen. You may wish to consult the following references in the New Testament: Colossians 1:18; Romans 9:25-26; I Peter 2:9-10 and I Timothy 3:15.

Q. How is the Church described in the creeds?
A. The Church is described as one, holy, catholic and apostolic.

These are the notes of the Church. They are to be found in the Creeds as follows:

One: Nicene
Holy: Apostles and Nicene
Catholic: Apostles and Nicene
Apostolic: Nicene

Q. Why is the Church described as one?
A. The Church is one, because it is one Body, under one Head, our Lord Jesus Christ.

At a practical level it is obvious that the Churches are not one. There are still several obstacles to full communion between the major families of Christians. These families are: Roman, Orthodox, Anglican and Protestant. Some would consider the Churches of the Anglican Communion to be a special family within Protestantism. Others, emphasizing that Anglicans have retained an apostolic succession of Ministry and Doctrine in common with the Roman and Orthodox traditions, would insist that it is a separate and distinct family. It is quite true that in England, the term, Protestant, has meant the religion of the established Church. It is also true that the full title of the American branch of Anglicanism is The Protestant Episcopal Church in the United States of America. This is because at one time Protestant meant non-Roman. The Churches of our Communion are Catholic, though non-Roman, and Protestant, though neither Lutheran nor Reformed. Although there are a number of differences in Faith and Practice, the relationship between all major families of Christians is better than it has been for centuries.

In another sense, the Churches are one, for they consist of baptized people who are members of the Body of Jesus Christ. They all acknowledge the headship of Christ. It is in this sense that the Catechism answers this question. One of our obligations is to pray and work for that practical unity that will express our oneness in Christ.

Q. Why is the Church described as holy?
A. The Church is holy, because the Holy Spirit dwells in it, consecrates its members, and guides them to do God's work.

It is obvious that the Church as a human institution, having us for members, falls short of the intention of God. If the Church were perfect, all of us would be excluded from membership. The point of the Catechism is that the Holy Spirit never gives up on the Church. He is always present, seeking to renew and reform. The capacity for renewal in the Church, seen over the long years of Church history, is one evidence of the divine origin of the Church.

Q. Why is the Church described as catholic?
A. The Church is catholic, because it proclaims the whole
   Faith to all people, to the end of time.

The word, catholic, means universal. We must never allow it
to mean only the Roman Communion. The word, ecumenical,
means universal also. It signified the whole of the inhabited
world. The Church is catholic in that it proclaims the whole
Faith to all people, at all times, and to the end of human
history. Although the Church will express the Faith within
the context of the culture and time in which it lives, it must
not be entirely captive to that culture and that time. It should
not be a Church for just one race, one nation or one social
class. The Church must be diversified enough to include "all
sorts and conditions of men" within its fellowship. This is
much easier said than done. At the same time it should be
said that there is nothing wrong with parishes attracting like
people, especially in those areas where there are a number of
congregations. In practice the Episcopal Church has been
rather more successful in such areas as the inner city than
many other mainline Churches.

Q. Why is the Church described as apostolic?
A. The Church is apostolic, because it continues in the teach-
   ing and fellowship of the apostles and is sent to carry out
   Christ's mission to all people.

First of all, the apostolic faith is content. It is the same good
news of Jesus Christ that was proclaimed by the early Church.
It is the offering of the same Sacraments. It is participation in
the same fellowship at the Altar, a fellowship shared with the
Lord and with one another. It is the fellowship of a Ministry
that goes back to the Apostles. It is customary to trace the
Anglican Ministry back to St. John at Ephesus, a source of the

orders of the old British Church. The apostolic mission is still the Mission of the Church. In this connection, please see the Great Commission, St. Matthew 28:18-20.

Q. What is the mission of the Church?
A. The mission of the Church is to restore all people to unity with God and each other in Christ.

The mission of the Church is defined by the Great Commission. This is a mission that is never completed, but one which must go on in every generation until human history ends.

Q. How does the Church pursue its mission?
A. The Church pursues its mission as it prays and worships, proclaims the Gospel, and promotes justice, peace and love.

St. Paul wrote: ". . . though we live in the world we are not carrying on a worldly war, for the weapons of our warfare are not worldly but have divine power to destroy strongholds. We destroy arguments and every proud obstacle to the knowledge of God, and take every thought captive to obey Christ . . ." (II Corinthians 10:3-5). The Church's weapons in the pursuit of its mission are also spiritual: prayer, worship and proclamation. This method is also its proper approach to the promotion of justice, peace and love.

Q. Through whom does the Church carry out its mission?
A. The Church carries out its mission through the ministry of all its members.

The Church carries out its mission through the work of its members just as any army carries out its mission through the work of its members. Our membership in God's Church is an enlistment in the army of the Lord.

CHAPTER XII

The Ministry

Q. Who are the ministers of the Church?

A. The ministers of the Church are lay persons, bishops, priests and deacons.

The mission of the Church belongs to all who are members of the Church. The Catechism reminds us that it is not just the Ordained Ministry that participates in the mission of the Church. Not all the members of the Church are bishops, priests and deacons, but all are ministers.

Another way of putting this would be to say that there are two Priesthoods within the Church. One is given by Jesus Christ to all members of his Body. The other, the Ministerial Priesthood, is a gift from Jesus Christ to his Body. The first priesthood is sometimes referred to as "the priesthood of all believers." There is nothing wrong with the phrase itself, but the doctrine has come to mean that each person is his own priest and needs no one else. This the Church does not believe. The doctrine of the royal priesthood of the Church does mean that we are one another's priests and can mediate the presence of God to one another and to the world outside the Church.

Q. What is the ministry of the laity?

A. The ministry of lay persons is to represent Christ and his Church; to bear witness to him wherever they may be; and according to the gifts given them, to carry on Christ's work of reconciliation in the world; and to take their place in the life, worship, and governance of the Church.

All of us are quite well aware that the Clergy represent the Church. In most instances, they, especially the regular parish clergy, are easily identified as the official representatives of the Episcopal Church in the community. The Catechism reminds us that the lay person is also a representative of Christ and his Church. Most people are aware of our affiliation with the Church. Whether or not that membership is important to us, whether or not we have respect and love for Jesus Christ, whether or not that formal loyalty has made a difference in the way that we handle both crisis and triumph will certainly be known to those who know us.

The lay person is under an obligation, according to the gifts given him or her, to carry on Christ's work of reconciliation in the world. The lay person's chief work will be in the world. This does not mean that the lay person's work will be more difficult that that of the Christian whose ordination implies work in the Church. The average parish priest will see much more sin and sordidness than the majority of his parishioners. It is true that the work of the lay person will take place in a different context than the work of the priest. Despite the inevitable compromises that are necessary in both Church and world, there is an obligation upon Churchmen to bear witness to the principles of Christ. It is no good to say that this is too idealistic, for it is the want of these principles that accounts for the sad situation that we are in.

The ministry of the laity takes place also within the life,

worship and governance of the Church. We are called to our own indispensable part in the common liturgy. To assist at the Eucharist by being present and by participating in the Service is part of the ministry of the laity. No Christian ought to be a mere observer of a Church Service. Each Christian has his own part. To understand this is to understand the difference between an audience, which assembles to observe and listen to a play or a symphony, and a congregation, which gathers to participate in worship.

The ministry of the laity is exercised in the life of the local congregation. Let us be aware that the local manifestation of Christ's Church depends upon the degree of our willingness to participate in the multitude of activities that constitute its life. There are those who will serve the Church in the diocese or national Church. Despite the high place of the ordained ministry in our Church, it requires the active participation of the lay order if it is to be loyal to its own constitution.

Q. What is the ministry of a bishop?
A. The ministry of a bishop is to represent Christ and his Church, particularly as apostle, chief priest, and pastor of a diocese; to guard the faith, unity, and discipline of the whole Church; to proclaim the Word of God; to act in Christ's name for the reconciliation of the world and the building up of the Church; and to ordain others to continue Christ's ministry.

The bishops began as pastors of a given city and surrounding areas. As the Apostles themselves died, the bishops became their successors in the leadership of the Church. The Episcopal Church retains the conviction of the undivided Church that bishops are the successors of the Apostles. This means much more than the succession of touch or the laying on of hands.

We do value the fact that our present bishops were ordained by bishops who were ordained by bishops and so back to the Apostles themselves. Another way of saying this is that our episcopate is not recently raised up as a decent provision for the administration of the Church, as is true in some Protestant Churches. Our bishops are a part of the historic episcopate. But this alone is insufficient. The bishops succeed the Apostles also by teaching the same doctrine and by doing the same work. The Apostles saw themselves as the proclaimers and interpreters of the Gospel. This is also the work of a bishop. A bishop is also the chief priest and pastor of a diocese. In the office of a bishop is the fullness of the ministerial priesthood. That is to say, he can perform every act that is necessary for the ministry to the Body of Christ. A priest or a deacon cannot ordain other priests or deacons nor can they confirm.

A diocese is the basic unit of the Anglican Communion. In the United States, the diocese is generally coterminous with the state. However, the larger states have several dioceses, and there are many dioceses which for reasons of geography include portions of two states. The basic unit within the diocese is the congregation. A congregation is either a parish or a mission. The parish is self-supporting. A mission receives partial financial aid. The diocese consists of parish and mission congregations in communion with it and the clergy who are canonically resident within it.

A bishop functions as the symbol of the unity of the Church and is the guardian of the faith, unity and discipline of the Church. The faith is defined by the Creeds and by the doctrine taught in *The Book of Common Prayer*. The unity of the Church is a unity in Christ, expressed in union with the General Convention of the Episcopal Church, which is a Church in fellowship with the Archbishop of Canterbury and other Anglican Churches. The discipline of the Church is to be found in canon law, the rubrics or directions of *The Book of Common Prayer*, and the customs of the Church.

Bishops join with other bishops in ordaining bishops. In order to continue the apostolic ministry, the episcopate is present in the person of at least three bishops at the ordination of another bishop. The rule of the Church since the Council of Nicea in 325 A.D. has been that this is the minimum number required to lay hands on a priest who is being elevated to the order of bishops.

It is the bishop who ordains priests. Other priests present join with him in the laying on of hands as a symbol of the collegiality of the priestly order. A deacon is ordained by the bishop alone.

Q. What is the ministry of a priest or presbyter?
A. The ministry of a priest is to represent Christ and his Church, particularly as pastor to the people; to share with the bishop in the overseeing of the Church; to proclaim the Gospel; to administer the sacraments; and to bless and declare pardon in the name of God.

The ministerial term, priest, is a contraction of the word, presbyter, meaning elder. An interesting aside is the development of the word. The intermediate stage is the word, prester, as seen in the medieval legend of Prester John. The Church still uses the older term, presbyter, in certain documents, such as the letters dismissory that transfer a priest from one diocese to another.

In a normal situation, the immediate pastor of a congregation will be the priest. His first duty is to proclaim the Gospel. This implies both the teaching and preaching of the Faith. He is to administer the Sacraments. It is the priest who will be the most usual minister of both Baptism and the Eucharist. Occasionally, a deacon may baptize in the absence of a priest. In an emergency any lay person may baptize. But normally it is the parish priest who does so. On occasion the bishop may celebrate the Eucharist for a given congregation. If there are any candidates for Holy Baptism, he will baptize them. Normally it is the parish priest who celebrates the Eucharist for his people. If these Sacraments are to be a regular part of the life of a congregation, the priest must administer them. He is the day to day pastor of God's people where they live. He it is who declares the good news of God's forgiveness to penitent sinners and pronounces blessing in God's name. These are never magical acts in which the universe is coerced through a formula to do men's bidding, but they are always religious acts which depend upon the response of penitence and faith to be fully effective.

A priest shares with his bishop in the overseeing of the Church. First of all, he exercises this responsibility in the local congregation. Secondly, he has a responsibility in the diocese, as a permanent member of diocesan convention. Informally, but more importantly, he is able to advise the bishop as one who is in close contact with the people.

There are some parts of the Anglican Communion where bishops and priests may be either male or female. Other portions follow the more ancient tradition of ordaining only men to these offices.

Q. What is the ministry of a deacon?
A. The ministry of a deacon is to represent Christ and his Church, particularly as a servant of those in need; and to assist bishops and priests in the proclamation of the Gospel and the administration of the sacraments.

The diaconate has a special ministry in its own right. In our Church the deacon is an ordained minister. Some other Churches have an elected diaconate, a lay office within the local church.

For Churches of catholic order, such as our own, the deacon is a member of a holy order of ministers. The diaconate is a ministry of service. The present custom in the Anglican communion is to use the diaconate as a probationary period for those on their way to the priesthood. There are a few Permanent Deacons who earn their living in secular work and serve the congregations where they live.

The deacon is called upon to be a servant of those in need. The Ordinal charges the deacon with this responsibility. It is to be hoped that the Church will find ways of restoring to the order this original function.

The deacon has a special function in public worship. At the Eucharist, the deacon reads the Gospel and assists the priest and congregation by serving as the administrator of the chalice. At other services, the deacon functions somewhat as any Lay Reader with the important exception that the deacon is able to preach sermons of original composition without further license.

Q. What is the duty of all Christians?
A. The duty of all Christians is to follow Christ; to come together week by week for corporate worship; and to work, pray, and give for the spread of the kingdom of God.

The practice of Christian duty is an evidence of Christian life. As Christians, as Churchmen, we have a number of duties. The first of these is a daily duty to follow Christ. This is a promise we made, or was made for us, at our Baptism. The second duty of a Christian is a Sunday duty, to worship. "To come together week by week for corporate worship" normally means Sunday. Following Christ means worshiping God. If we do not wish to follow Christ, there will be few occasions upon which the Church can compete with other interests. If we wish to follow a golf ball on Sunday mornings rather than follow Christ, we will doubtless do so; but let us have no rationalizations about being able to find God in the open air rather than in a church. God chooses to come as Bread and Wine among those who are gathered in his Name. If we do wish to follow Christ, we will join him where he has said that he will be.

Anglican Churches have generally avoided the strict Sabbatarianism that has characterized certain religious groups.

There are those who have to work on Sunday. This is to be regretted, for Sunday ought to be a day for worship, rest and recreation. We would be much better off as a society if Sundays were free from weekday pursuits. However, the Churchman who has to work during the hours of worship is not guilty of sin if he makes a reasonable effort to worship God at some time. Remember that the early Christians were not free to enjoy Sunday as a day of worship and rest until the Roman Empire became friendly to the Church in the fourth century, A.D. These Christians went to the Eucharist early Sunday morning and then to their work. Let those who must work on Sunday in our time attend an early service if possible. There are other opportunities for worship in the average Episcopal Church. Some have daily services. Some services are either early in the morning or after normal working hours. Most of our clergy would be glad to have more weekday services if more people would attend. If such services are not available, it is possible in many parishes to make arrangements to receive Communion from the Reserved

Sacrament in a private service.

We do need a regular rule about receiving the Eucharist. The three times a year that is required in order to be counted as a communicant in good standing is a bare minimum. It is a rule that is intended to give the priest some kind of standard to use when making up the annual report. Even then, it is not the only standard for measuring our standing in the Church. We are expected also to worship God every Sunday in his Church in order to be counted as in good standing. In any case, if we are following Christ we will have far exceeded any kind of rule with regard to the number of communions made.

Our duty is also "to work, pray, and give for the spread of the kingdom of God." This is a continuing duty. Jesus called us to be workers. We ought to work both in the Church and in the world for the spread of the rule of God. Jesus called us to pray. He taught that we should pray and never give up. Finally the Lord called us to give. A large percentage of his teaching had to do with stewardship and the use of money. A bishop once told a congregation that there were four books that a Christian ought to use. These were the Bible, the Prayer Book, the Hymnal, and the checkbook! That is sound advice.

CHAPTER XIII

Prayer and Worship

Q. What is prayer?

A. Prayer is responding to God, by thought and by deeds, with or without words.

One of the things which distinguishes mankind from the balance of the animal creation is prayer. Men instinctively seek to address a higher power than themselves.

The essence of prayer as the Christian Faith understands it is *response.* It is the Church's conviction that prayer would not take place if God himself did not take the initiative. Prayer includes both thought and deeds, when both are offered to God. Most prayer makes use of words, although there is a level of prayer where words are absent.

Q. What is Christian prayer?

A. Christian prayer is response to God the Father, through Jesus Christ, in the power of the Holy Spirit.

Christian prayer is a relationship with the Holy Trinity. Such prayer is a response to God the Father through Jesus Christ who is God the Son. Our Lord said that we are to pray in his name. You may wish to look up St. John 16:23-24 in this connection. The Name of Jesus Christ is not a formula that is tacked onto prayer. To pray in the Name of Jesus Christ is to understand the One to whom we pray as defined by Christ's revelation of the nature of the Father. To pray in the Name of Jesus Christ sets forth the content of prayer as that which is consistent with the revelation of God in the Person of Jesus Christ. In this kind of prayer, the Holy Spirit is particularly active in our behalf. You may wish to read of the role that St. Paul assigns to the Holy Spirit in our prayers (see Romans 8:26-27).

Q. What prayer did Christ teach us?
A. Our Lord gave us the example of prayer known as the Lord's Prayer. *See page 364.*

The version of the Lord's Prayer that is used in the Church's worship is found in St. Matthew 6:9-13. A second version of the Lord's Prayer is in St. Luke 11:2-4.

The Catechism directs our attention to a page in the Book of Common Prayer, in the second rite of the Holy Eucharist, where the two English translations of the Lord's Prayer from St. Matthew are set side by side. The first version is based on the translation made in the King James or Authorized Version of the Bible. The second, a more contemporary translation, is based on the work of the International Consultation on English Texts (ICET), a commission that is attempting to provide a common translation of certain texts that are used in the worship of English speaking Churches. The New Testament original is in the Greek language. The words of Our Lord himself were in Aramaic.

We note that the Lord's Prayer assumes that the one who prays is a member of a corporate fellowship, the Church. It is "Our Father" not "My Father" who is addressed. The prayer was given to the Apostles and is most appropriate to those who are in fellowship with Christ's Church.

The Lord's Prayer is used in common worship, and it occurs at the high point of any service. Note that it follows the Prayer of Consecration at the Eucharist and precedes the collects at Morning and Evening Prayer.

In our service this prayer normally concludes with a doxology:

For thine is the kingdom,
    and the power, and the glory,
For ever and ever. Amen.
	For the kingdom, the power,
	    and the glory are yours,
	now and forever. Amen.

A comparison of this with any modern translation of the Bible will show that the doxology is not in the original text. The doxology was not added until some time in the second century. Anglican and Protestant Churches, deeply influenced by texts that were used for the translation of such Bibles as the Authorized Version use the doxology. However, in *The Book of Common Prayer* the Lord's Prayer is said in its shorter form in such services as the Great Litany, Compline and in An Order of Service for Noonday.

The Lord's Prayer is a fitting part of our private devotions. At the beginning it is an outline of that for which we ought to pray. At the conclusion, it is a summary of our prayers.

Q. What are the principal kinds of prayer?

A. The principal kinds of prayer are adoration, praise, thanksgiving, penitence, oblation, intercession, and petition.

While it may not be necessary to a vital prayer life to be aware of the formal divisions of prayer, it may be quite helpful to be so. Such knowledge may lead us to a better balance in our private devotions. The Catechism provides an exposition of each of the seven main types of prayer.

Q. What is adoration?
A. Adoration is the lifting up of the heart and mind to God,
   asking nothing but to enjoy God's presence.

Adoration is the enjoyment of God by thinking upon him. It
is a pure form of the love of God. Adoration does not require
many words. It is a form of prayer that is achieved by most
who do attain to it with great effort. We most naturally lapse
into either petition or intercession or both. If we have diffi-
culty in sustaining this form of prayer, we should remember
that a church is a natural setting in which to practice the quiet
adoration of God. It is also most helpful to think about God
in the presence of the Reserved Sacrament in those churches
in which the practice of reservation is followed.

Q. Why do we praise God?
A. We praise God, not to obtain anything, but because God's
   Being draws praise from us.

The logical result of the adoration of God is the praise of
God. Both the Prayer Book and the Bible abound in the
praise of God. Adoration and praise are two unselfish forms
of prayer.

Q. For what do we offer thanksgiving?
A. Thanksgiving is offered to God for all the blessings of this
   life, for our redemption, and for whatever draws us closer
   to God.

The Catechism bids us thank God for the blessings of this life,
both material and spiritual. God is the source of every good
and perfect gift and ought to be thanked for them. He is the
source of our redemption, and our thankfulness ought
always to be a thankfulness that includes the Cross and the

One who was the Saving Victim. Let us remember to thank God for whatever and whoever draws us closer to himself.

It is not only the good and pleasant things of life that draw us closer to God. Many times we are closer to God precisely because we have gone through sad, trying and even evil experiences. While we do not thank God for evil, we can thank God for the opportunity that has been provided for drawing closer to him.

Q. What is penitence?

A. In penitence, we confess our sins and make restitution where possible, with the intention to amend our lives.

The word, "repent" means to turn around and go in the opposite direction. Sorrow for sins or contrition is a necessary part of penitence but only a part of it. Confession of sins, either privately to God, or to God in the presence of a priest who is empowered to declare God's forgiveness frees us to receive the power of God to amend our lives. The opportunity for private confession is available in the Episcopal Church. Please see the two forms for the Reconciliation of a Penitent included in *The Book of Common Prayer* (pages 447-452). Such private confession to a priest is available, not required. The Anglican rule on this kind of confession has been, "All may; some should; none must." The priest is bound by the seal of the confessional. He must never disclose the contents of a confession to anyone; nor may he discuss it with the penitent, without asking and receiving permission to do so.

The Catechism teaches that where possible we are to make restitution. This would be a clear obligation where the sin has involved a financial loss to another.

Q. What is prayer of oblation?
A. Oblation is an offering of ourselves, our lives and labors, in union with Christ, for the purposes of God.

In Holy Eucharist I, it is stated that Christ made upon the cross "by his one oblation of himself once offered, a full, perfect, and sufficient sacrifice, oblation, and satisfaction, for the sins of the whole world." The oblation of Christ was the total offering of himself to God. In our oblations we offer the totality of ourselves in union with his perfect oblation.

Q. What are intercession and petition?
A. Intercession brings before God the needs of others; in petition, we present our own needs, that God's will may be done.

Intercession, bringing the needs of others before God, is one of the more important things that we can do for others. We must be careful not to prescribe what God ought to do for them. Although there may be description of specific circumstances in our prayers as a means of intensification in prayer, we should remember that the purpose of prayer is not to give information or direction to the Almighty. The goal of prayer is that God's will be done, and we know that that will is goodness itself.

Petition, bringing our own needs to God, is a legitimate form of prayer, for God wills us so to pray. Some would scorn this form of prayer as being too selfish. The omission of petition may be a symptom of spiritual pride, however. When we say, "I am so spiritual that I would not stoop to praying for my own needs," we have adopted an attitude which implies superiority to our brothers and sisters in Christ. That attitude defeats the Christian life in us. God expects us to pray for ourselves. The opposite error to the above is to pray only for ourselves and to neglect adoration, praise, thanksgiving, penitence, oblation and intercession. The secret of Christian prayer is balance.

Q. What is corporate worship?
A. In corporate worship, we unite ourselves with others to acknowledge the holiness of God, to hear God's Word, to offer prayer, and to celebrate the sacraments.

Most of what has been written before has been directed to our personal prayers. However, much that has been said is applicable to corporate worship.

In corporate worship, prayers tend to be formal in that in the Episcopal Church most public prayers follow a set form and are printed in a book to be read by the Minister and Congregation. These prayers are common prayer, approved by the Church, available to all and shared by all. Because they are in this form, we are spared much of the danger of having to join the Minister in his or her private devotions. We are somewhat sheltered from the personal moods of our leaders in worship. The morning coffee may have been bitter, the toast burned or there may have been a family fight, but the words of the prayers will be those of faith, hope and love. We may not be able to do much about the tone of voice, but the words, at least, will be Christian words.

The Catechism teaches that no one is a Christian alone. We are Christians only as a part of the Body of Christ, which is his Church. To worship means to acknowledge worthship. This we do together. We acknowledge the holiness of God. Having done so, we are free to hear God's word both written in the Holy Scriptures and interpreted in the Sermon. We join in corporate worship to offer the prayers of the Church, which are better balanced than our private prayers will ever be; and to celebrate as a community the presence of God with us as he acts in the Sacraments.

CHAPTER XIV

The Sacraments

Q. What are the sacraments?

A. The sacraments are outward and visible signs of inward and spiritual grace, given by Christ as sure and certain means by which we receive that grace.

We live in the world of the outward and visible and the world of the inward and spiritual at the same time. For this reason God does not hesitate to use the outward and visible to both signify and convey the inward and spiritual grace of his presence. All sacraments have an outward and visible sign. They are the appointed means by which we receive an inward and spiritual grace. They are sure and certain means of grace in that Christ has appointed them, and we may always trust them as conveying that which they signify.

Q. What is grace?

A. Grace is God's favor towards us, unearned and undeserved; by grace God forgives our sins, enlightens our minds, stirs our hearts, and strengthens our wills.

The grace of God is a common phrase in the New Testament and is frequently mentioned in the ritual of the Church. Grace is God's favor toward us, exercized not because of any intrinsic merit in us but because of his own great love. We can never earn God's favor. It is a gift that is freely given. Grace does four things: forgives our sins, enlightens our minds, stirs up our hearts and strengthens our wills. Every sacrament, if received in faith, has this four-fold consequence.

Q. What are the two great sacraments of the Gospel?
A. The two great sacraments given by Christ to his Church are Holy Baptism and the Holy Eucharist.

The Dominical Sacraments, that is to say those instituted by our Lord himself during his earthly ministry, are Holy Baptism and the Holy Eucharist. The first is the sacrament of initiation, without which no other Christian sacrament is effective. The second is the sacrament of nourishment. Physically we are born once. That is unrepeatable. Holy Baptism is unrepeatable. We eat and drink regularly in order that our physical life may be nourished. We make our communions regularly in order that the life of God within us may be nourished.

Baptism can never be repeated. Any Christian Baptism that is in water and in the Name of the Father, Son and Holy Spirit is valid. One exception that should be mentioned is baptism by any cult that considers the Holy Trinity to be three separate and distinct persons. If there is any doubt as to either the fact or the validity of any baptism, then the person ought to be given conditional baptism. There is a form for conditional baptism in the Prayer Book on page 313 at the conclusion of the Baptismal Office.

In an emergency, that is to say when the person to be baptized is in danger of death, any baptized person may administer baptism using the form that is provided in the Prayer Book. Such baptism is to be reported to the priest so that the baptism may be recorded. If the person who is baptized recovers, the baptism is celebrated at a public service with only the baptism in water omitted.

The Eucharist is repeatable. It is the Church's custom that the laity receive but once on any given day. This rule is to hinder any superstition concerning the benefits of the Eucharist and the way they are obtained. It is that we receive the Body and Blood of Christ in the Eucharist and not the amount of Bread and Wine that is important. Attendance at later Marriage Eucharists, Burial Masses and Ordinations provide exceptions to this general rule, of course.

A priest who celebrates at more than one Eucharist on a given day will have to make his communion each time he celebrates. The traditional limit on the number of Eucharists that a priest may celebrate in one day is three. If the priest is the celebrant at one Eucharist and then assists at another (unless it is a concelebration), he would not make a second communion at the second service.

CHAPTER XV

Holy Baptism

Q. What is Holy Baptism?

A. Holy Baptism is the sacrament by which God adopts us as his children and makes us members of Christ's Body, the Church, and inheritors of the kingdom of God.

Our Christian life begins with our baptism. There are many temptations to locate the beginning of the Christian life elsewhere. That elsewhere is very often the place and time where we have begun to respond to God's love. We may say that we began our Christian life when we joined the Church, and that is correct, unless we mean that we joined the Church when we were confirmed. On the other hand, we may be tempted to say that the Christian life began at our conversion. It may well be that years after we have received the grace of Holy Baptism, or even some time before we choose to be baptized, our love for God and our awareness of his love for us were awakened in a marvellous way. An authentic conversion experience is a great blessing. It can occur in many ways and at different times of life and circumstance. God deals with each one of us as individuals. Rightly we value a conversion experience if it is a good one and produces in us a healthy relationship to God, the Church and other people, but the beginning of our Christian life is bound up with Holy

Baptism. That is where God begins the Christian life in us.
Once we are baptized, we are Christians. We may be Christians who are growing spiritually or Christians who are dying
spiritually. Often we are Christians whose spiritual growth
has stopped and does not begin again until our love for God
is consciously reawakened. Be that as it may, our Christian
life begins with God's action in Holy Baptism.

The Catechism says that God adopts us as his children.
This is Scriptural language. You may wish to see Romans
8:23 and Galatians 4:5 in this connection. Christ is the only
begotten Son of God. We are God's children by adoption and
by grace.

In Holy Baptism, God makes us members of Christ's Body,
the Church. The New Testament makes frequent reference to
the idea that the Church is the body of Christ and that we are
members of that Body. Please see the following Scriptures: I
Corinthians 6:15; 12:27; Ephesians 1:23; 5:29-30;Colossians
1:18 and 2:19. These are all quotations from St. Paul. Our
Lord used a different picture with the same meaning. He said,
"I am the vine, and you are the branches" (St. John 15:5). The
idea is that as we live in Christ, we extend his life in the world
today.

If we are the sons and daughters of the Most High God,
then we are inheritors of the kingdom of God. The ancient
Jews thought of this kingdom as the sphere of God's rule.
That rule took place in three dimensions. God was the ruler
of all nature: "Heaven is my throne and the earth is my
footstool" (Isaiah 66:1). God will be the ruler of the future,
the kingdom that is coming. In this regard you may wish to
consult the following references: Isaiah, chapters 11-13 and
34:1-8; Obadiah 1:15-21; Micah 4:1-8 and Zephaniah 3:8-13.
This is the time when God will triumph over all opposition
and evil, and his kingdom will be in the midst of all people.

This is the time to which the New Testament looks forward as the time in which "The kingdom of the world has become the kingdom of our Lord and of his Christ, and he shall reign for ever and ever" (Revelation 11:15b). God is also the ruler of the individual who takes upon himself the yoke of the kingdom. It is this third sense that relates the kingdom of God to the present through our obedience.

Q. What is the outward and visible sign in Baptism?
A. The outward and visible sign in Baptism is water, in which the person is baptized in the Name of the Father, and of the Son, and of the Holy Spirit.

Essential to Holy Baptism is water. The Church allows both immersion, which is rare, and pouring, which is common. Nothing may be substituted for water, which symbolizes both cleansing and birth. Although some early Christian baptisms may have been in the Name of Jesus, St. Matthew 28:19 directs that Baptism is to be in the Name of Father, Son and Holy Spirit. It may be noted that all who have been baptized in services that take their wording from the King James Version of the Bible will have been baptized in the Name of the Father and of the Son and of the Holy Ghost. Holy Ghost is an older English form for saying Holy Spirit. It is still used in Rite I services.

Q. What is the inward and spiritual grace in Baptism?
A. The inward and spiritual grace in Baptism is union with Christ in his death and resurrection, birth into God's family the Church, forgiveness of sins, and new life in the Holy Spirit.

In Baptism, we are united with Christ. As he died; so we also die to the old life, which is life unaided. As he rose again; so we rise to the beginning of a new life which is aided by his grace. Baptism is our birth into God's family, the Holy Catholic Church. All sins committed before Baptism are forgiven in it. The Holy Spirit is then enabled to work in us.

Q. What is required of us at Baptism?
A. It is required that we renounce Satan, repent of our sins, and accept Jesus as our Lord and Savior.

We all make promises. A promise may be as simple as the promise to pay all utility bills by the due date. This is necessary if we are to have power and water and telephone. A promise may have all of the dimensions of the vows we take on our wedding day.

The first promise that is required of us at Baptism is a renunciation. We are to renounce Satan. In tradition, Satan is a fallen angel. This legend reminds us that evil is a corruption of good. Lust is love gone wrong. Gluttony is the healthy appetite that has become the unhealthy passion for food. Pride is the normal feeling of self-worth that has become a monster. A cancer is a formerly good cell that is running wild. Satan, sometimes called the Devil or Lucifer, stands for all that corrupts good and frustrates the design of God. Satan is also known in Scripture as "the deceiver of the whole world" (Revelation 12:9). Evil is a shortcut to nowhere. It delivers something quite different from that which it promises to deliver. When we become Christians, we renounce this deception. We renounce the desires that participate in such deception. All desires are not sinful. The Christian faith does not consider the renunciation of desire to be the pathway to salvation. We promise to turn our backs on those desires that are destructive of good. That is the literal meaning of repentance: to turn our backs and march in the opposite direction.

We also promise a positive action. We accept Jesus as our Lord and Savior. This most important promise has to do with the most important Person, Jesus Christ. This promise has to do with commitment to and trust in this Person. The Church does not ask us for blind faith. We may discover who Jesus is by a careful and prayerful reading of the Gospels. You may wish to begin with the Gospel according to St. Mark, which has the virtue of moving rapidly through the essentials. It is also the shortest and earliest of the Gospels.

When we accept Jesus Christ as our Savior, we also accept him as our Lord. The final baptismal promise has to do with following him and obeying him.

Trust, also called faith, may be a conviction dearly held by the mind and the mind alone, or it may be conviction plus an attitude of life that results in action. Our beliefs are important and even essential, but unless they lead to commitment and action, the process of faith has been prematurely arrested. As the New Testament reminds us, ". . . faith by itself, if it has no works, is dead." (St. James 2:17). The Prayer Book teaches that our trust is not simply a conviction that Jesus is Lord, nor is it this and the good feeling that comes from the conviction, but it is all this and a willingness to follow and obey. Jesus is Savior, and he is Lord and Master as well.

Q. Why then are infants baptized?

A. Infants are baptized so that they can share citizenship in the Covenant, membership in Christ, and redemption by God.

In the beginning, Christianity was an appeal to adults. However, with these adults came children. It was not long before people asked, "Are our children part of the Church?" Were these children of Christians to be considered Jewish or pagan,

or were they part of Christ's kingdom? The Church an-
swered, "Let them be baptized." It is inconceivable that
Christianity with its roots in Judaism and the idea of the
Covenant could exclude the children of Christian parents
from the benefits of religion.

Q. How are the promises for infants made and carried out?
A. Promises are made for them by their parents and sponsors,
   who guarantee that the infants will be brought up within
   the Church, to know Christ and be able to follow him.

The responsibility for the religious education of children falls
primarily upon the parents. To assist them the Church provides for sponsors or Godparents.

   Originally, sponsors were those who recommended adult
inquirers for Baptism and membership in the Church. The
background of this was the attempt of the pagan Roman
government to infiltrate the congregations and to secure
information that would be used to crush the Christian
movement. It became necessary for the Church to require
that inquirers have someone already within the Christian
community testify that the convert's motivations were genuine
and that the inquirer was not a Roman police spy.

   With the recognition of the Faith by the government, the
office of sponsor began a transition. For many centuries the
sponsor has been a Godparent. It is the sponsor who answers
for the child in the Baptismal Office. In a real sense, we feel
free to baptize the child and use the sponsor's faith in lieu of
the faith of the child. It is proper that the parents join with
friends as sponsors. Together they guarantee to the Church
that the child will be brought up within the Church. This is
not the kind of guarantee that is enforceable in the courts. It
is a solemn promise on the part of both parents and God-

parents, and it is one for which they will be accountable before God. Whether the child will be able to know Christ and be able to follow him will depend upon a number of factors, parents, church and the person himself; but the spiritual atmosphere for such knowledge and obedience is correctly described by the Catechism.

CHAPTER XVI

The Holy Eucharist

Q. What is the Holy Eucharist?

A. The Holy Eucharist is the sacrament commanded by Christ, for the continual remembrance of his life, death and resurrection, until his coming again.

The earliest written account of the institution of the Eucharist is not in the Gospels, but rather it is in the first letter of St. Paul to the Corinthians, the eleventh chapter. There our Lord is recalled as saying to the Apostles, "Do this in remembrance of me." He also said, ". . . as often as you eat this bread and drink the cup, you proclaim the Lord's death until he comes."

Therefore, the celebration of the Eucharist is according to Christ's command. The Eucharist or Holy Communion is often spoken of by Churchmen as "the Lord's own Service." It is the only Christian worship service that he instituted. Other Services of the Church are either adaptations of Jewish Services or have been developed to meet specific Christian needs.

The Eucharist is a remembrance, but it is not just a memorial. The background of the Eucharist is the Passover. That event in the history of Israel was not so much remembered as it was summoned from the past into the present. In it every Israelite knew himself to be one who had come out of

Egypt. It is at the Eucharist that Jesus and his disciples join us and we stand at the Cross and the empty Tomb. This the Church shall do until time ends and the Lord comes again.

Q. Why is the Eucharist called a sacrifice?
A. Because the Eucharist, the Church's sacrifice of praise and thanksgiving, is the way by which the sacrifice of Christ is made present and in which he unites us to his one offering of himself.

The word, Eucharist, means thanksgiving. In it, the Church offers God its own sacrifices of praise and thanksgiving. The one, perfect sacrifice of Christ is made present and the sacrifices of the Church are united with his total offering of himself and presented to the Father.

Q. By what other names is this service known?
A. The Holy Eucharist is called the Lord's Supper, and Holy Communion; it is also known as the Divine Liturgy, the Mass, and the Great Offering.

The Lord's Supper is a common term among most Protestant Churches and has been included in previous additions of the American Prayer Book. The Holy Communion has been the more common term among Anglicans for the entire Service, although the most recent Prayer Book restricts that term to the liturgy of the table itself. The word, liturgy, means work, and so the Eastern Church most often describes the Eucharist as the Divine Liturgy. Mass has been used by the Roman Communion and is not uncommon in Anglican conversation about the Sacrament, although no Prayer Book has contained the term for centuries. Mass is a reference to the dismissal of the people at the conclusion of the Service. The Great Offering refers to the consecration itself.

Q. What is the outward and visible sign in the Eucharist?
A. The outward and visible sign in the Eucharist is bread and
   wine, given and received according to Christ's command.

The proper matter of the Eucharist is bread and wine.
Nothing may be substituted for either. Bread may be leavened
or unleavened. Commonly it comes in wafer form, although
some parishes may prefer to bake the bread in loaf form. The
wine may be any true grape wine, although it is customary to
avoid types that contain carbonation.

Q. What is the inward and spiritual grace given in the
   Eucharist?
A. The inward and spiritual grace in the Holy Communion is
   the Body and Blood of Christ given to his people and received by faith.

The personal influence upon our lives is the real presence of
Christ given in the Eucharist. Christ is there. We receive what
is given by faith. Without faith the reception of the Eucharist
is not only worthless, it is destructive. In this connection,
please see I Corinthians 11:27.

Q. What are the benefits which we receive in the Lord's
   Supper?
A. The benefits we receive are the forgiveness of our sins, the
   strengthening of our union with Christ and one another
   and the foretaste of the heavenly banquet which is our
   nourishment in eternal life.

The Catechism lists three benefits of receiving the Eucharist.
The first is the forgiveness of our sins. This assumes a penitent
heart. The Sacraments are never magical. Their effectiveness
in us depends upon our response to what Christ offers in

them. The second is communion with Christ and his Church. The Communion has not only a God-ward dimension but also a horizontal thrust toward our brothers and sisters in Christ. The Communion also looks forward to eternity, where we shall be in union with Christ and the Church Triumphant.

Q. What is required of us when we come to the Eucharist?
A. It is required that we should examine our lives, repent of our sins, and be in love and charity with all people.

The Presence of Christ in the Eucharist is real, regardless of our own worthiness. Whether the Eucharist does us any good depends upon our own preparation for participation in this Sacrament. Self-examination, leading to repentance, and love and charity for all people is required by the Catechism.

The increased frequency of communions in our own time has been a mixed blessing in that the seriousness of preparation has declined. Few Churchmen, especially among the Clergy, would dispute the historical fact that the Eucharist is the norm for Sunday worship. Some would say that other Services are better suited to reaching people who are not yet committed to Christ and his Church. Some would also say that fewer communions and better communions, prepared for beforehand, would be of greater benefit to both the individual and the Church. It is important for us to know that we need not make our communion every time we are present at the Eucharist. If we are not to make the action useless and even detrimental to our own spiritual growth, we ought to go forward to the altar rail only when we are prepared to do so.

This does not mean that we have to be perfect in order to receive the Sacrament. The Church and the Table are for sinners only. It may well be that those times when we are especially conscious that we have failed our Lord, our neighbors and ourselves are the times when we need the communion most. We may be better prepared when we come because of conscious need than at many other times. The point that must be made is that the casual communion, made with little or no preparation, is spiritually dangerous.

CHAPTER XVII

Other Sacramental Rites

Q. What other sacramental rites evolved in the Church under the guidance of the Holy Spirit?

A. Other sacramental rites which evolved in the Church include confirmation, ordination, holy matrimony, reconciliation of a penitent and unction.

The reference is to what is sometimes termed the lesser Sacraments. Strictly speaking the Sacraments are Holy Baptism and the Holy Eucharist, the Dominical Sacraments. The five listed in the answer above are sacramental rites, derived from Apostolic or later Church practice. These share with the Sacraments of the Gospel both outward and visible signs and inward and spiritual graces.

Q. How do they differ from the two sacraments of the Gospel?

A. Although they are means of grace, they are not necessary for all persons in the same way that Baptism and the Eucharist are.

Holy Baptism is the sacrament of initiation. One does not become a Christian without Baptism. The Eucharist is necessary for all Christians in the same way that meals are necessary for all human beings. It is the sacrament of nourishment. The sacramental rites are for Christians only in certain circumstances or states of life. For example, unction is for a Christian who is sick. When the Churchman is in good health, that particular rite would make no sense at all.

Q. What is Confirmation?
A. Confirmation is the rite in which we express a mature commitment to Christ, and receive strength from the Holy Spirit through prayer and the laying on of hands by a bishop.

Confirmation is based on Apostolic practice. In this connection you may wish to read Acts 8:14-17. Before the emergence of large numbers of baptized children in the Church, Confirmation was closely associated in time with Baptism. With an increase in numbers of children who had received the Sacrament of Baptism in infancy, Confirmation was separated by some years from the time of Baptism.

The rite of Confirmation is an expectation of the Church for all Christians. The precise age of Confirmation is now seen as a pastoral matter, but the Prayer Book anticipates that it will be at a time when a mature commitment to Christ can be expressed. In our branch of the Church, Confirmation is administered by a bishop.

Q. What is required of those to be confirmed?
A. It is required of those to be confirmed that they have been baptized, are sufficiently instructed in the Christian Faith, are penitent for their sins, and are ready to affirm their confession of Jesus Christ as Savior and Lord.

Baptism is requisite for admission to all Christian sacraments. Before Confirmation, instruction in the Faith, normally either by or at the discretion of a priest, is provided. Those to be confirmed should be both penitent for their sins and ready to make explicit their belief and trust in Christ as both Savior and Lord. Confirmation instruction should provide a thorough grounding in basic beliefs as stated in the two great creeds of the Church and *The Book of Common Prayer*. Because of the explicit requirement that those confirmed be penitent for their sins, this is a good time for the priest to instruct in the matter of confession.

Q. What is Ordination?
A. Ordination is the rite in which God gives authority and the grace of the Holy Spirit to those being made bishops, priests and deacons, through prayer and the laying on of hands by bishops.

Ordination is the setting apart by the laying on of hands of those who are to serve the Church in one of the three Sacred Orders of Ministry. The authority of Christ and the grace sufficient for the office conferred are bestowed in this action.

Ordination is an excellent example of a sacramental rite that is not for all Christians. Less than one percent of the members of the Church will ever need or experience the grace of Holy Orders. Such Orders are a state of life to which not every Christian is called.

Q. What is Holy Matrimony?
A. Holy Matrimony is Christian marriage, in which the woman and man enter into a life-long union, make their vows before God and the Church, and receive the grace and blessing of God to help them fulfill their vows.

Matrimony existed long before the Christian Church. It is a

sacrament of the natural order. The Church does not look upon marriages contracted before civil magistrates or ministers of non-Christian religions as in any degree inferior or less binding than Christian marriage. However, for members of the Church, the sacramental rite, Holy Matrimony, is provided. Marriages in the Church are explicitly life-long in intention. Vows are taken before God and in the presence of the Church. The outward and visible sign of Holy Matrimony is the giving of rings and the joining of hands. The inward grace of Holy Matrimony is the blessing of God to help the couple fulfill their vows.

It should be stated that the Church has a Service for the Blessing of a Civil Marriage, whereby those who have been married by a judge may have their marriage blessed. This is particularly helpful for those who may become active in the Church some years after they have been married. The Church does not presume to remarry them, but it will add the Blessing to their already valid marriage.

Q. What is Reconciliation of a Penitent?

A. Reconciliation of a Penitent, or Penance, is the rite in which those who repent of their sins may confess them to God in the presence of a priest, and receive the assurance of pardon and the grace of absolution.

The declaration of forgiveness to penitent sinners is based on St. John 20:23 and St. Matthew 16:19 and 18:18. It is probable that confession was originally in the presence of the congregation. Private confession developed because public confession provided gossips with so much material! The formularies of worship of the Anglican Communion assume that private confession is especially needed by those who are dying, or who are unable, because of a troubled conscience, to make their communions. In addition, there are many Churchmen, both clergy and laity, who make private confession a part of their own rule of life, with great spiritual benefit. The general rule in the Episcopal Church concerning private confession is that, "Some should, all may, but none must."

In addition to the rite of Penance, the absolution of sinners is a regular part of the ministry of bishops and priests and is exercized most frequently in the declarations of forgiveness in the Eucharist and Morning and Evening Prayer. Confession, whether public or private, is the remedy for sins committed after Baptism. The priest declares what God has promised the penitent, the good news that they are forgiven.

Q. What is Unction of the Sick?

A. Unction is the rite of anointing the sick with oil, or the laying on of hands, by which God's grace is given for the healing of spirit, mind and body.

There are two forms of Unction. The anointing of the sick with blessed olive oil is of apostolic origin. You may wish to read St. James 5:14ff. in this connection. The alternate form is the laying on of hands for the sick. This was a regular practice of our Lord's disciples.

The intention of Unction in either form is for the healing of the mind and spirit as well as the body.

Q. Is God's activity limited to these rites?

A. God does not limit himself to these rites; they are patterns of countless ways by which God uses material things to reach out to us.

The Church does not consider God to be limited to the Sacraments or sacramental rites. His activity is in nature, in history and in persons. These rites are special means of his activity in the Church. We may be sure that God works there. We do meet him in many other places and persons as well.

Q. How are the sacraments related to our Christian hope?
A. Sacraments sustain our present hope and anticipate its future fulfillment.

Sacraments are tokens of God's presence in the day in which they are received. They are also promises of his triumph in the Day that is to be. Thus the Sacraments and sacramental rites sustain us in the present and point to the fulfillment of God's work in us and in history.

CHAPTER XVIII

The Christian Hope

Q. What is the Christian hope?

A. The Christian hope is to live with confidence in newness
and fullness of life, and to await the coming of Christ in
glory, and the completion of God's purpose in the world.

The Catechism concludes with the theme of hope. The logic
of what has gone before leads to hope. Those who hope can
live in confidence that their creed will prove true. The
Christian hope is designed to produce a life that is new in that
it is different from the life that lacks the dimension of faith.
Properly understood, the Christian faith and its consequent
hope produce fullness of life rather than constriction. Our
Lord said, "I am come that they might have life and have it
more abundantly" (St. John 10:10b).

Hope is the ground of patience. Patience does not mean in-
difference to the tensions and terrors of the present world.
Patience does not mean discharge from the necessity of doing
something to correct as many present evils as we can correct.
The patience that is born of hope does mean that we wait for
Christ in whom is the completion of God's purpose in the
world. Bishop Terwilliger reminds us that Christ is the content
of Christian hope:

> . . . Christian faith does not expect or give any

answers about the future or eternity or the end of
the world that cannot be found in the person of
Christ — that cannot be found in him as a *person.*
It might be put this way: the eschatology of the
Christian faith is the 'therefore' of the resurrection
of Christ.

The word 'eschatology' is necessary for an understanding of what we are talking about. It comes
from the Greek word, *eschaton,* which means
'end.' It is not the kind of end to be found in the
end of a string, or at the end of one's rope, a termi-
nus. It is the kind of end which we think of when we
say, 'What end do you have in mind' or 'With this
end in view . . .' It is a purposeful end, a fulfillment, or perhaps best of all, a consummation.
When Christians speak of Christ as 'the Alpha
and the Omega,' the Beginning and the End, we
mean that Christ is the consummation.[3]

Q. What do we mean by the coming of Christ in glory?
A. By the coming of Christ in glory, we mean that Christ will
   come, not in weakness but in power, and will make all
   things new.

The first coming of Christ in Jesus of Nazareth was as a
human being, with the limitations of humanity. Jesus was
liable to hunger, thirst, temptation, death. The second
coming of Christ will be with all of the power that belongs to
him by right. "He will come again in glory to judge the living
and the dead, and his kingdom will have no end" (Nicene
Creed, BCP, pages 327 & 359). The Scriptural basis for the
statement that Christ will make all things new is Revelation
21:5.

---

[3]Robert E. Terwilliger, *Christian Believing,* New York: Morehouse-Barlow Co.,
1973, p. 106.

Q. What do we mean by heaven and hell?
A. By heaven, we mean eternal life in our enjoyment of God;
   by hell, we mean eternal death in our rejection of God.

The Bible often uses analogies for spiritual realities. The term, heaven, originally referred to the upper part of the universe, and we still use it in that sense, when we speak of "the heavens." In Hebrew thought, it is the place of the abode of God, although it is to the credit of Solomon that he realized that "the heaven of heavens cannot contain thee . . ." (I Kings 8:27. KJV).

By heaven the Church means a state rather than a place. Heaven has come to mean eternal life, which is not only a matter of duration but also a matter of quality.

The word, hell, originally meant the hidden place. Hela was the Norse goddess of the dead. Earlier English versions of the Bible use the word, hell, to translate a single Hebrew word and two quite different Greek words. The Hebrew word, Sheol, has as its rough equivalent, the Greek word, Hades. Both stood for the place of the dead. It is in this sense in which the traditional English translation of the Apostles' Creed understands Christ's descent into hell, i.e., the place of departed spirits. The other Greek word is Gehenna, a biblical word which signifies a place of punishment. It had a local, precise reference. Near Jerusalem was the Valley of Hinnom, a site of child sacrifice during Old Testament times (II Kings 23:10), and thus, a place of abomination. In the time of our Lord, the Valley of Hinnom was the city dump of Jerusalem. It was associated with waste, uselessness and uncleanness. By the first century, Gehenna had become the word that stood for the fate of those who had suffered eternal death in their rejection of God. The association of fire with hell came from the constant burning at the city dump. Hell is the opposite of the enjoyment of God. In Hell we cannot enjoy God, for we have rejected him.

Q. Why do we pray for the dead?
A. We pray for them, because we still hold them in our love, and because we trust that in God's presence those who have chosen to serve him will grow in his love, until they see him as he is.

There is a distinction between praying for the dead and praying to the dead. Furthermore, it is not for all the departed that the Church prays. It is for the faithful departed in Christ that our prayers are offered. This is because they and we are members of the Church. We would not feel it to be odd to be asked to pray for other members of the Church. Why should it be unusual to pray for members of the Church who are departed? The Church consists of three parts: the Church Militant here on earth, still fighting the world, the flesh and the devil; the Church Expectant, in Paradise, and the Church Triumphant, in heaven, beholding God as he is. In so far as the faithful departed are growing in the love of God, they may be benefited by our prayers.

This does not mean that the absence of our prayers will diminish the reward of the faithful by anything other than the benefit of the expressed love of the Church Militant. God will accomplish his purpose in them whether we pray or not. However, it seems consistent with Christian love and not inconsistent with Scripture to continue our prayers for them, and, in addition, to believe that they pray for us, who have so much more need for prayer.

Q. What do we mean by the last judgment?
A. We believe that Christ will come in glory and judge the living and the dead.

That there will be a final judgment is the clear teaching of the New Testament. In this connection you may wish to read St. Matthew 16:27; 25:31-46; Acts 17:31; I Corinthians 6:3; II Peter 2:4; Jude 1:6 and Revelation 20:9b-10. These Scriptures teach the judgment of both men and angels.

It is Christ who will be our judge. He is the best qualified, for Jesus Christ is both God and Man. As God, Christ both knows everything and is perfectly just. As Man, Christ knows what we have to face and is wholly merciful.

Q. What do we mean by the resurrection of the dead?
A. We mean that God will raise us from death in the fullness of our being, that we may live with Christ in the communion of the saints.

The Christian Faith is fundamentally Hebrew rather than Greek in its attitude toward the future life. The Greek thought of the survival of the soul. In some Greek thought this involved the survival of the intelligence. Rather than speaking of the survival of the soul, the Jews taught that God would provide a body for the righteous. This was a later development in the Jewish religion. It was the position on the future life held by the Pharisees and opposed by the Sadducees.

It is interesting to note that while our Lord clashed with the Pharisees on many matters, he was one with them in a belief in the resurrection of the body. You may wish to read St. Mark 12:18-27 and St. Luke 20:27-39 in this connection.

St. Paul also identified with the Pharisees rather than the Sadducees in the question of the resurrection of the dead. See Acts 23:6 for this identification. In his one prolonged discussion of the matter, I Corinthians 15:12-58, St. Paul makes clear that he does not mean to equate resurrection with mere

resusitation of a corpse. He teaches that God provides a
spiritual body appropriate to eternal life. The resurrection of
the dead is life in the fullness of being, personal, identifiable
and whole.

Q. What is the communion of saints?
A. The communion of saints is the whole family of God, the
   living and the dead, those whom we love and those whom
   we hurt, bound together in Christ by sacrament, prayer
   and praise.

It is Christ who unites his people in one communion, the
living and the dead. For a sense of the closeness that the early
Church felt for the departed, see Hebrews 12:1,23. The focal
point of the communion of saints is the Lord's Table where
we join our praise "with Angels, and Archangels, and with all
the company of heaven . . ." (BCP, pages 334 & 362). We
shall live with Christ and in the communion of the saints.

Q. What do we mean by everlasting life?
A. By everlasting life, we mean a new existence, in which we
   are united with all the people of God, in the joy of fully
   knowing and loving God and each other.

Everlasting life possesses both duration and quality. It is a
new existence in which we shall realize perfect love of God
and love of one another. In this love there will be full knowledge of both.

Q. What, then, is our assurance as Christians?
A. Our assurance as Christians is that nothing, not even
   death, shall separate us from the love of God which is in
   Christ Jesus our Lord. Amen.

The answer to the Catechism's final question is a summary of Romans 8:31-39. A reading of that passage will prove the best commentary on this question. St. Paul begins by asking, "If God is for us, who is against us?" The list of enemies may be long and always includes death, but God is stronger than any of these, including the final enemy.

Amen is Hebrew and means, "So be it!" or "I agree!" It is said by the congregation at the conclusion of a prayer offered by the Minister on behalf of the Church. It means that each person who says, "Amen," assents to the prayer. The Catechism calls for our assent to the whole Christian Faith, a commitment of mind and heart to the Lord and to the Gospel. Both the Catechism and this commentary offer a great deal of information, but the information is given with an end in view, your lifelong commitment to Jesus Christ in the fellowship of his Church.